about this pamphlet

One of the main ambitions of **research** in **practice** is to make it easier for local authorities and voluntary organisations to access reliable research, distilled and translated with a particular audience in mind. This series of research reviews covers key practice areas, identified by practitioners, and key research strategy issues, identified by planners and policy makers. The work and methods of **research** in **practice** chime well with the developing national agenda to build more effective, multi-professional and multi-agency services for children, in part by creating and using reliable research evidence.

Sometimes we review research on work that is already experienced as problematic by those seeking to help troubled children and families. Our last two reviews are examples of that. This review comes from another direction – seeking to bring a somewhat hidden issue into the light, examining it and considering how the knowledge identified here might influence the future direction of services. Parenting as such has, rightly, gained increasing prominence over the last few years – but the parenting support needs of disabled parents have been largely ignored. It is particularly timely to consider this subject: it is important in its own right; it is a good example of the need for professionals to work across agency boundaries; and it opens up for the non-researcher important questions about research objectivity and judgement.

So, this review has two aims. First, to bring together the research literature on disabled parents and, second, to set that research within the context of the policy and practice thinking of its time. The authors reveal the subjectiveness of much of the research and the way in which it is often 'the creature of its time'. It shows how, as our societal attitudes change, so do the approaches of professionals, including researchers. The coverage of the welcome dialogue about 'young carers' also demonstrates the way in which research is negotiated and mediated.

QUALITY MARK This review has been peer-reviewed by a range of academics based in universities and service agencies, and by practitioners and others seeking to assist the development of evidence informed practice. We are grateful to them for their generosity and good advice. What follows here has benefited enormously from their wisdom: Sean Atkinson, Christine Ballinger, Colin Barnes, Tim Booth, Wendy Booth, Liz Brown, Sheryl Burton, Elizabeth Cooke, Hilary Corrick, Richard Cotmore, Pam Cowley, Mike Fisher, Ray Jones, Bill Joyce, Annie Knight, Enid Levin, Sal Lodge, Sue McGaw, Hugh McGlaughlin, Jill Manthorpe, John Newland, Tony Newman, Michael Power, Sue Rodrigues, Nicky Stanley and Simon Unsworth.

Celia Atherton
Director of **research** in **practice**

contents

introduction

Providing support for parents to help them bring up their children better is at the core of the Government's family policy. However, many disabled parents feel that this is still only a pipe dream for them. (Goodinge, 2000)

defining disabled parents

It is important to clarify at the outset how we are defining disabled parents for the purpose of this review. Although it is crucial to the welfare of children that all parents are well supported, much evidence has emerged over the past decade pointing to the fact that it is very hard for parents with chronic illnesses, physical and/or sensory impairments, Deaf parents, those with learning difficulties, those with particular mental health needs and those with drug or alcohol related issues, to access information, resources and support to help them fulfil their parenting responsibilities. This has had serious implications for the welfare of large numbers of families.

These groups of parents are collectively described in this review as disabled parents. It should be pointed out, however, that not all these groups of parents – and indeed not all of the individuals involved in the consultation – would use the term 'disabled' to describe themselves. For example, many Deaf activists make a deliberate and political point in distancing themselves from the term, believing that it implies an inappropriate judgement of their cultural and linguistic experience.

The term disabled parents is used in this review to describe systematic disadvantage rather than to describe personal or group characteristics. Where a wide range of parents (broadly identifiable as disabled parents) are coming up against similar problems in relation to the way in which services and support are organised, such an inclusive definition helps to clarify just what it is in the nature and structure of organisational responses that may constitute a barrier to these groups of parents. It also helps to identify unaddressed gaps in services and to question the operation of unexamined assumptions on the part of service providers. There are also instances where identifiable groups of parents are at a particular disadvantage or where a particular specialist input becomes more relevant. These can be highlighted without losing sight of the links between groups.

need for statistical information about disabled parents

It is worth noting that in spite of all the research discussed in this review that has a bearing on the lives of disabled parents, the number of disabled parents in the UK is entirely unknown at this point. In the absence of dedicated statistics, numbers have to be extrapolated from data drawn from population surveys collected for other purposes (Goodinge, 2000).

In spite of the lack of specific, statistically based information, there is widespread agreement that there has been an increase in both the number of disabled parents and in their visibility as a sub-section of the parenting population (Wates, 1997). Nonetheless, disabled parents, and those working alongside them to improve services and support, find that the lack of data and consequent invisibility of disabled parents creates a number of difficulties, some of which are practical and some of which have more to do with research status.

The administrative 'invisibility' of disabled parents has certainly contributed to the difficulty of planning and providing appropriate specialist information, health and social services to disabled adults in their parenting role (Goodinge, 2000). It makes it less likely that parenting needs will be considered in relation to the employment, living benefits and housing needs of disabled people. At the same time, the low profile of disabled parents means parenting support needs are not routinely assessed and addressed. It also hinders access (and the understanding of the need for access) to mainstream parent support information, goods and services. For example, the Disability Pregnancy and Parenthood International (DPPi) information service reports that the lack of quantitative information makes it difficult to persuade manufacturers that there is a potential market for specialised equipment to assist disabled parents. Grant making bodies and charitable trusts want to know potential numbers that an initiative will reach and can be reluctant to fund a statistically 'invisible' group.

For all these reasons, statistically based information about the situation of the groups of parents discussed in this report is needed. A relatively straightforward way to access this information would be by including questions in the next census to make it possible to determine the numbers of disabled parents (including foster, step and adoptive parents) with dependent children defining themselves as having a long term illness or impairment, mental health issue or learning difficulty.

At the same time, it is important to look beyond the desire for numbers in order to address the legal and rights contexts. A large-scale survey, costing millions and highlighting disabled parents, could have the undesired consequence of further problematising these groups of parents rather than keying them more effectively and routinely into mainstream parent and family supports. It is perfectly feasible to identify and address the impact of the barriers without knowing how many people are involved.

Goals do not in themselves determine outcomes and, in reality, the impact of research is notoriously unpredictable. The involvement of disabled parents in planning, execution, evaluation and dissemination at least gives a better chance of avoiding research that is, at best, irrelevant to meeting the needs of disabled adults and their children and, at worst, contributes to the systemic disadvantages they face. Generally speaking, and all the more so in relation to family life, the experience of impairment cannot be seen as a fixed variable but rather as something that is liable to change in both foreseeable and unforeseeable ways in relation to everything else that is going on within a family. Partners, and children too, move between different welfare and health categories from time to time, while particular medical and social labels may become somewhat arbitrarily fixed to individuals. The relative impact of different conditions varies in relation to the changing situations of family members, while all individual and family changes take place within broader economic and social contexts that can, in large part, determine access to any additional resources that might be needed (Wates, 2003).

research assumptions regarding disabled parents

How, then, do we develop support systems that are accessible, welcoming and geared up to the needs of all parents including those with physical and sensory impairments, with learning difficulties, users of the mental health system, parents dealing with drug and alcohol related issues, Deaf parents, and disabled parents from black and minority ethnic communities?

Research is not value neutral. In this review, we show that assumptions (often unexamined) in relation to parenting undertaken by disabled adults have influenced the formulation of research aims, its design, interpretation and impact upon policy and practice. In particular, we examine how some of the existing research has proved a misleading guide to understanding disability in relation to family life and delivering effective and timely support to adults and children.

Much of the research with a bearing on the family lives of disabled people begins from the assumption that disability is a personal characteristic – whether physical, intellectual, emotional or sensory – that, to a greater or lesser extent, causes problems for the disabled person and for those who live with them. In so far as this research has a social dimension, it is concerned with evaluating the psychosocial adjustment of the family unit.

From this perspective, the presence or absence of external supports and the nature of relationships with service providers are not seen as determining outcomes, but as indicators of the extent to which families have or have not come to terms with difficulties related to the presence of individual impairment (Ferguson et al, 2000).

In line with this body of research, the development of services in the statutory and voluntary sectors has often focused on assessing the 'capacity' of the disabled adult to parent successfully. At the same time, too little attention has been paid to the organisational, economic and attitudinal contexts within which parenting takes place and the impact that these have on a disabled adult's attempts to carry out their parenting responsibilities successfully.

Minimising the negative impact of parental impairment becomes the focus, rather than supporting the parent to uphold the welfare of the child. Within this frame of reference, the child comes to be seen as the primary client within the family while the support needs of the disabled adult in relation to parenting remain unaddressed.

The review goes on to evaluate how a more holistic and emancipatory approach to supporting disabled adults with parenting responsibilities is being developed by many researchers, informed by a more structural understanding of disability. We argue that such an approach is compatible with the need, identified by the Social Services Insectorate (SSI) (Goodinge, 2000), to work from within an understanding of both adult community care and children's legislation when supporting families in which one or both parents are disabled.

who is the review intended for?

This review is aimed at managers and practitioners with strategic, operational and training responsibilities for delivering support to disabled adults and their children. If it is to be effective, work that is more consciously oriented towards support calls for the development of co-ordinated practice across adults' and children's services and between a range of relevant agencies in both the voluntary and statutory sectors, including maternity services, specialist adult and children's social services, area child protection committees, education, health, leisure, transport and housing.

It is a time of change and some uncertainty for agencies working on behalf of disabled parents and their families. While services to disabled adults continue to be linked more closely with health, locating children's and adult services in separate central government departments has become a significant trend. It includes the creation of Children's Trusts as a key co-ordinator of services to children. Seizing the opportunity for planned working across several agencies is more important than ever (Jones et al, 2003).

contents of the review

Following this introduction and a brief section on how the review was conducted, we identify and review the existing research on disabled parents and 'young carers' by outlining three perspectives within disability related research. These we characterise as Personal, Ecological (in the sense of including social and physical environments within the examination of family life), and Organisational. These are far from watertight and exclusive categories, however. Indeed, we suggest that much of the work that stems from an ecological or organisational perspective on the experience of disability in families is still, in reality, somewhat narrowly focused on personalised perceptions of disability.

The final section looks at the emergence of a body of research in which disabled people themselves have an integral role. This is based in the social model of disability and is explicitly committed to the identification and removal of barriers constraining the full social participation of disabled people in familial roles, including parenting.

As might be imagined, the potential literatures to consider are extensive. The aim is not to conduct a systematic review but rather to illustrate the perspectives discussed through reference to a limited number of representative texts. The impact of these trends in research is also explored with reference to key policy documents.

Since the publication of *A Jigsaw of Services*, based on an SSI inspection of services to support disabled adults in their parenting role (Goodinge, 2000), the significance of which we discuss, several organisations have held events linked with the issue of disabled parents. These research based seminars and workshops were variously organised by SSI regional committees, **research in practice**, Making Research Count (based at York University) and the Centre for Evidence-Based Social Services (in the South West). They were attended by personnel from between a third to a half of local authorities, including those representing adults' and children's disability services, children and families, carers and young carers' services, health, education and the non-governmental family support sector.

Although there was widespread agreement among participating professionals about the need for change, the potential for more effective family support and the linkage with a number of key government social agendas (including promoting independence, preventative agendas, support for families, partnership working and the promotion of direct payments), there was also frustration on the part of many of those attending at the difficulty of establishing joined-up working across different divisions of social services and between agencies. These seminars guided our decision to include a legislative overview exploring adult and children's legislation in relation to supporting disabled parents and their children (see Appendix). We hope that this, and the checklist of questions for local authorities and other relevant agencies which ends this review (see p47), will be useful to local authorities and other agencies working to improve planned services to disabled adults with parenting responsibilities.

how we conducted the review

From the outset, we felt that this review demanded a particular approach to gathering and synthesising 'evidence'. Our argument throughout is that 'disabled parents' is not an area of research that lends itself to conventional systematic review methodology. This is because we question the assumptions about disability underpinning much existing research. It is, therefore, more important to outline these assumptions and to help readers develop a critical awareness of their impact on policy and practice than it is simply to convey 'the evidence' as if it represented an established body of uncontested knowledge about the parenting provided by disabled people.

Our approach has been threefold.

- We have drawn together the knowledge of research, policy and other work that, as experienced researchers in this field, we have accumulated over a number of years. Our concern has been to illustrate the importance of the theoretical approaches to disability adopted by researchers from different perspectives and 'traditions'; therefore, we have guarded against selection bias by the deliberate inclusion of a large number of studies and papers from which we would distance ourselves theoretically and politically.

- We have tried to respond to the concerns expressed by members of **research in practice** attending seminars that we have facilitated. This has included the incorporation of knowledge about research, policy and other work that they have brought to such events.

- We have sublitted successive drafts of this review to a rigorous and on-going process of peer review that has helped extend its coverage and accuracy, and has involved scrutiny of the document (in terms of content, structure and style) by a group of people with a keen eye on how such a review could meet the needs of its intended audience.

models of disability research

personalised understandings of disability

Much of the research into disabled people's parenting is steeped in a model which regards disability as a personal characteristic and links any presenting problems to individual impairments, mental health status or learning difficulty rather than with the social context and environment in which parenting takes place. This can be seen not only in the way in which severity of impairment is given a central explanatory role (for instance, in the use of Intelligence Quotient as a proxy for parental ability), but also in the way in which parents are grouped into impairment-specific categories for the purposes of research (Roy, 1990). A search of the literature reveals titles such as *Psychosocial adjustment of adolescent children of a depressed, arthritic or normal parent* (Hirsch et al, 1985), *Depressed and non-depressed mothers with problematic pre-schoolers: attributions for child behaviours* (White and Barrowclough, 1998), and *Attachment patterns in children of depressed mothers* (Radke-Yarrow, 1991). Within this tradition, impairment is seen as the paramount variable, outcomes for children are the focus of examination and interventions to protect children from the adverse impact of parental disability are the proposed solution.

linking particular impairments to parenting outcomes

In some studies, researchers have looked for the effect of a particular impairment, or even feature of impairment, on children's well-being and behaviour. For example, Jamison and Walker (1992) found that the emotive expression of pain on the part of parents was a strong determinant of illness behaviour in children themselves. However, their research did not extend to the context in which people experiencing severe pain seek to parent, by looking, for example, at issues such as medication, methods of pain relief in the context of parenting dependent children, the availability of support, the attitudes of outsiders, or the availability of counselling and peer support.

Brandt and Weinert (1998) studied 174 families recruited through the United States Multiple Sclerosis (MS) Society, and found that children were most at risk of developing mental health related problems where parental MS was accompanied by marital disagreement and a lack of financial resources. However, this did not lead the authors to discuss the financial and other support that parents (and therefore children) might benefit from; rather, the focus is on interventions aimed at the children in these families.

Similarly, Wang and Goldschmidt (1994) describe a study in which 50 consecutively admitted psychiatric inpatients were interviewed about their parental responsibilities, and in which around a quarter of children were described as having emotional problems. Again, the focus of this study is solely on clinical intervention aimed at improving parent-child relationships rather than on the social and other support that parents and other family members might require. In addition, it lacks a comparative design that would make it possible to compare the proportion of children having emotional problems where parents were not admitted to hospital or in the population generally.

Although outcomes for children frequently focus on mental health and 'well-being', studies have also looked at outcomes in terms of physical harm. For instance, LeClere and Kowalewski (1994), in their study of the effects on children of any other member of the family being disabled, found that when both parents were disabled there was a significant increase in the risk of injury, accident and poisonings on the part of children. Little attention is given to additional barriers likely to be faced by families in which both parents are disabled; for example, the increased likelihood of unemployment and attendant poverty, the shortage of accessible housing, and the increased difficulty, therefore, in providing a safe environment for children.

Roy (1990), in his review of studies of physically disabled parents, makes the general point that studies are often characterised by the small samples of disabled parents involved (Dowdney and Skuse, 1993), and because studies concentrate almost exclusively on the experiences of mothers as opposed to fathers. Limitation in the design of these studies is in the nature of the samples chosen, as well as the methods used to identify and recruit participants. Andron and Tymchuk (1987), in a now somewhat dated review of research into parenting with learning difficulties, argue that studies have generally failed to control for social class, and that a causal link between intellectual impairment and poor parenting cannot therefore be made.

skewed samples

A further difficulty in interpreting research findings is the tendency for studies to include parents already known to services, thus skewing the sample towards one with identified 'problems' sufficient for some sort of state intervention (Campion, 1995; Booth and Booth, 1994a; Wates, 1997):

> Most professionals who come into contact with families where there is a disabled parent are likely to do so because the family is in need – those who are coping well are not observed. (Campion, 1995)

There is a dearth of research into the context in which the majority of disabled people and, for that matter, non-disabled people, parent – that is, one that is not dependent on such families being 'known to services', 'in need', or users of 'young carers' projects. It is as though failure and difficulty are of more interest to researchers than success, which is unfortunate since an analysis of the factors that make for success are of crucial importance in developing effective parent and family support systems.

the socio-economic context

Research adopting a personalised model of disability has generally paid insufficient attention to controlling for the effects of broader socio-economic disadvantage on the ability of people to parent successfully. In other words, researchers have been quick to identify associations between impairment and poor parenting without adequately considering the role of poverty, inaccessible housing and other expressions of material disadvantage. An exception is a recent study from the US that looked at outcomes for child and marital adjustment in families with a spinally injured mother. A range of psychometric tests were carried out on 88 mothers with spinal cord injuries (and their families), as well as on 84 non-disabled mothers (and their families) closely matched in terms of age, ethnic background, education and income (Alexander et al, 2002). Virtually no differences in outcomes for the two groups were detected once these other variables had been taken into account. While the study is still squarely from a personalised perspective (in so far as it is concerned with a sample defined by impairment and focuses on the possibility of negative outcomes for the children), it does indicate that when the socio-economic context is controlled for, the differences usually ascribed to impairment are not apparent.

organisation and attitude

Studies have focused attention on presumed inadequacies in parenting by disabled people, while at the same time failing to address or even to pay much attention to the organisational and attitudinal issues that the data often raise.

Booth and Booth (1994a) argue that the removal of children into public care has traditionally been seen as prime facie evidence for neglect, without due consideration of the structural barriers that parents with learning difficulties in particular may have had to face in their attempts to secure support. In the examples discussed by the Booths, parents had often had little or no access to support and information that would significantly increase their chances of successful parenting. A common outcome was family breakdown and the separation of the child(ren) from parent(s).

Many such parents were themselves raised in institutions and have, therefore, grown up without familial role models, with restricted opportunities to learn parenting skills (for instance, through baby-sitting in adolescence) and in a climate that sought to undermine rather than support their aspirations of having and raising children. Nevertheless, the tendency has been for this background to be ignored in studies identifying the children of learning-disabled parents as 'at risk'.

> Parents were not given an opportunity to demonstrate their capacity to look after the child... (Booth and Booth, 1994a)

We will discuss the importance of the Booths' (and others') work on supporting parents with learning difficulties later.

in summary

Much of the literature on disabled parents has the following characteristics:

- an assumed correlation between parental impairment and a negative impact on children's well-being as the main focus
- impairment is seen as the only, or the most relevant, variable of interest
- research recommendations tend to be directed towards direct interventions involving children.

These assumptions are emphasised over the social, familial and wider economic contexts within which parenting takes place and the nature of the supports available to disabled parents. The result is that parents and parenting become explicitly or implicitly identified as problematic. While this body of research goes back a long way and appears rather dated in the light of the more contextualised approaches to studies of parenting discussed below, it is worth pointing out that it is still well represented in recent studies, particularly in more clinically-oriented literatures (see, for example, Steck, 2000).

We also argue that the assumptions identified above remain in much of the work in the 'ecological' tradition and even in some of the work that we have broadly described as being concerned with 'organisational' factors or contexts.

ecological: social and physical environments

This section looks at a body of research that has had a much greater concern for environmental factors and how these may facilitate parenting or else render it more difficult. This is potentially an important literature in relation to parents in that it might be expected to broaden research interest out beyond preoccupation with personal characteristics and presumed 'deficits' of parents with particular impairments, to include consideration of the socio-economic context in which disabled adults carry out their parenting responsibilities. We argue, however, that in so far as it has been applied to the situation of disabled parents, much of this work retains a focus on impairment and parenting 'deficit', although it has moved towards placing this within social contexts.

We will look at the background to ecological perspectives on parenting, and then discuss this model in relation to work on parenting and mental health, the *Framework for the Assessment of Children in Need and their Families* (Department of Health, Department for Education and Employment and Home Office, 2000), broader research on parenting support (which largely excludes the perspective of disabled parents), the literature on resilience, and the body of research concerned with 'young carers' that has developed over the last decade.

'Ecological' approaches to parenting have their roots in broader theories of human, and especially child, development put forward by Bronfenbrenner (1979). With respect to parenting, the most influential work has been carried out by Jay Belsky and colleagues (Belsky et al, 1984; Vondra and Belsky, 1993). These authors argue that successful parenting depends not on any one factor but on the interaction of a range of factors, including the individual attributes of parents, the attributes of children, the nature of intra-family relationships, the sources of stress and support within and outside the family, as well as the broader socio-economic context in which the family lives. Indeed:

> Social networks, as well as formal services, play an influential, but still largely unexplored, role in the development and maintenance of competent parenting. (Belsky et al, 1984)

The interaction of these factors is often placed within a life-course perspective which recognises that parenting, and the stresses and supports influencing parenting, will change over time.

research linking parenting and mental health

It is significant that the vast majority of the research studies in this area centre around mental ill-health, with a concentration on examining the impact of conditions such as depression, 'personality disorders' and drug and alcohol dependence as contra-indications for children's welfare. Centrally important in this respect has been the work of Cleaver and colleagues (1999), both in documenting the 'impact' of parental ill-health on children's development and by influencing the development of policy and practice.

Coming under the spotlight in this way has had mixed consequences for parents as users of the mental health or drug and alcohol related systems. In addition to any positive benefits in terms of resource allocation and policy development, it can be argued that it has unduly problematised the parenting of these adults. Parents, and also children themselves, fear that this will stigmatise their families with the result that the identification of any support needs in relation to parenting will become tied in with child protection measures and could lead to the children being removed from home.

Since these are very much the fears that disabled parents in general, and not just those mentioned above, express in relation to service interventions (Goodinge, 2000), we make no apologies for exploring this literature around diagnosis of mental ill-health and parenting capacity at some length. Furthermore, its implied relevance to parents with physical, cognitive and sensory impairments and learning difficulties is reflected, as we show below, in key policy initiatives around supporting children and families.

The following quotations illustrate the attachment to a personalised perspective on parenting capacity that is still frequently apparent in the work of those adopting an ecological perspective in relation to parenting and perceived mental ill-health:

> It is unlikely that an individual who is caught up with his or her own psychological concerns will have the ability to decentre and take the perspective of a dependent infant. Without the psychological resources to understand, and consequently tolerate, the daily demands and frustrations of an infant or young child (let alone a teenager), a parent will be hard pressed to demonstrate the patience, sensitivity and responsiveness that effective parenting requires. (Vondra and Belsky, 1993)

Similarly,

> Regardless of the specific defining characteristics of such disorders as schizophrenia, borderline personality, generalized anxiety, and depression, the presence of mental illness suggests that psychological resources for parenting may be compromised or absent altogether.
> (Vondra and Belsky, 1993)

Indeed, the authors go on to assert that while child attributes, social support and personal capacity to parent are all important, it is the latter which is the most significant of all (Belsky et al, 1984). An ecological approach, so influential in the thinking behind current policy and practice, is markedly reticent as to the relative place of impairment, mental health status, drug and alcohol dependence and learning difficulty on the one hand, and structural and organisational factors on the other, in determining parenting outcomes.

An influential body of work has seen parental disability in terms of the risk factors associated primarily with child neglect, but also with child abuse. Once again, the focus has primarily been on parents with diagnoses of mental ill-health, and the literature is underpinned by often-cited research showing the high number of fatal child abuse cases where one or both parents were regarded as experiencing mental health related problems. For instance, Falkov (1996) found that parental 'psychiatric disorder' was present in 32 of the 100 fatal child abuse cases he studied. Similarly, James (1994) found that six of the 30 fatal child abuse cases he studied involved mental ill-health on the part of the parent. It is also underpinned by a large body of work showing the significant proportion of children 'looked after' (Quinton and Rutter, 1984; Isaac et al, 1986; Bebbington and Miles, 1989) and on child protection registers (Gibbons et al, 1995; Thoburn et al, 1995) who have parents who are mental health system users.

The work of Sheppard (1997 and 2002) on maternal depression is of importance in this tradition of research. Sheppard, in a study of the relationship between maternal depression and child abuse, in which 116 mothers were interviewed, found that:

> The really marked differences between families with abused children and those not abused was where maternal depression was present.
> (Sheppard, 1997)

The policy and practice messages that emerge from Sheppard's work focus on the importance of working with mothers and addressing their depression as a crucial factor in reducing the risk of their children experiencing some kind of neglect or abuse. In addition, he argues that a focus on domestic violence is required given the frequency with which this group of women report having experienced it – a point made by Stanley and Penhale (1999) as well.

Furthermore, Sheppard acknowledges the disabling effect that child protection proceedings may have, in and of themselves, on the capacity of mothers to fulfil their parenting responsibilities:

> The experience...of being subject to child protection procedures is not likely to engender a feeling of self-confidence and well-being on the part of many mothers. (Sheppard, 1997)

Similarly,

> The effects of these [child protection] investigations on women already wracked by the effects of depression may be even more severe, and in some circumstances inhibit the very parenting capacities which practitioners are ultimately attempting to encourage. (Sheppard, 1997)

However, two important limitations to the study are the absence of consideration of the role of fathers in these families (whether as mental health service users themselves, as sources of potential support for depressed mothers, or as perpetrators of abuse), and the decision to look at the presence or absence of depression only in the mothers of children identified as experiencing abuse, and not among the population of depressed mothers of non-abused children. Failure to consider the experience of the majority of depressed parents who do not abuse their children is an important omission since it is here that information about social, organisational and personal factors that increase the likelihood of successful parenting will be found.

The place of parental depression as a risk factor for child neglect is an important feature of a number of studies funded by the Department of Health in the early 1990s and published in an overview document called *Child Protection: Messages from Research*, more commonly known as the 'Blue Book' (Dartington Social Research Unit, 1995). This programme of work was inspired to a large extent by the reaction to the Cleveland child abuse 'scandal' of the late 1980s and the perception that a concentration on child protection activities had inhibited the provision of suitable, preventative, family support. Parton (1997) discusses a key finding, arising out of the study by Thoburn and colleagues (1995):

> With the exception of a few severe assaults and some sexual maltreatment, long-term difficulties for children seldom follow from a single abusive event or incident - rather they are more likely to be a consequence of living in an unfavourable environment, particularly one which is *low in warmth and high in criticism*. (Parton, 1997; original emphasis)

This served to refocus attention on the mental health status of parents (and especially mothers) and on the implementation of family support measures enshrined in the Children Act 1989 which, it was claimed, had become submerged in a system overflowing with, and dominated by, the processing of child protection enquiries. The result of this was that parents entering the child protection system often reported being offered little by way of support (Gibbons et al, 1995). Parental illness, and particularly mental ill-health, was also a significant issue in the children studied in later research into the impact of the Children Act 1989 (Aldgate and Bradley, 1999; Brandon et al, 1999; Tunstill and Aldgate, 2000). Significantly, what a number of these studies showed was that:

> In cases where parental limitations had led to care proceedings...parents often felt that they were 'prejudged and condemned', and that there was little recognition of the stresses they were under or their desire to contribute as much as they could to their children's lives. (Aldgate and Statham, 2001)

These studies caution us not to see the experiences of parents with diagnoses of mental ill-health as separate and unique in relation to other parents. The Children Act studies referred to above show how families most at risk of seeing their children enter public care are those experiencing multiple disadvantage and chronic dysfunction which may, or may not, include mental-health related difficulties alongside drug and alcohol issues, violence, partnership instability, physical impairment and ill-health, racism and a range of socio-economic difficulties. It is important to recognise that many families with non-disabled parents also experience profound social exclusion and that the unavailability of supportive services is not experienced by disabled parents alone.

Crossing Bridges

The identification of mental ill-health as a risk factor for child abuse and neglect, and the considerable attention paid to the issue as a result, has had mixed consequences for these and, we would argue, other groups of parents.

It led directly to the production of *Crossing Bridges* (Department of Health, 1998), a training pack that has been generally welcomed as a valuable resource, though arguably it is not widely known and used (Kearney et al, 2000). *Crossing Bridges* materials are intended to provide a comprehensive approach to working in holistic and cross-agency ways with parents who are mental health service users and their children. These materials adopt a clear ecological perspective, with an emphasis on the personal capacity of 'mentally ill' parents, the developmental needs of children, and the social environment and broader economic and structural context in which families live. They are sensitive to the close reciprocal links between parenthood and mental health, including both an awareness of the potential impact of pregnancy and birth on mental well-being for mothers and the importance of an adult's experience of being parented when a child. The materials provide an exhaustive review of the literature with relation to parenting and mental health which is beyond the scope of this publication but which the reader may want to consult.

These materials could be criticised, however, for placing too much emphasis on diagnoses and labels relating to mental ill-health, and outlining potential effects on parenting, at the expense of addressing the social disablement that parents with such diagnoses frequently experience in terms of stigma and prejudice, as well as reduced income and financial security (for a full critique see Tanner, 2000). It is significant that discussion of the legislative and policy context devotes considerably more space to the provisions of the Mental Health Act 1983 and the Children Act 1989, and their related codes of practice and guidelines, than to the NHS and Community Care Act 1990. Legislation relating to direct payments and the potential for promoting choice and control on the part of parents who are mental health service users is not mentioned.

the Framework for the Assessment of Children in Need and their Families

The Framework is the major practice guidance intended to implement the Children Act 1989 in relation to the process of assessment and the development of more holistic styles of working with family need. Although it is explicitly presented as being informed by an ecological approach, we would argue that the encouragement to examine 'wider environments' is not applied consistently. As suggested earlier, preoccupation with the assessment of parental capacity and the assumed vulnerability of their children, extends not only to parents with mental ill-health diagnoses and/or drug and alcohol related issues but also to parents with 'serious health problems or impairments'.

While the right words are often said about the need to address socio-economic inequalities, the policy and practice response within an 'ecological' perspective has nonetheless remained focused on the personal characteristics of these parents, with the service issue seen largely in terms of the assessment of parenting capacity. This is epitomised by the influential work by Cleaver and colleagues (1999) on parental mental ill-health and its impact on child development. This work ultimately rests on an assumption that impairments affect parental capacity, which in turn affects children's developmental needs – social factors are seen as having the potential to aggravate these impacts but do not alter the fundamental assumption.

The next quotation illustrates the tendency in those sections where the focus is disabled parents, to turn from environmental and organisational issues that clearly have implications for support and to locate the origin of the problem in the parents themselves:

Some parents may have serious health problems or impairments, which may place upon children responsibilities inappropriate to their years unless informal support and appropriate services are provided for the family, in consultation with the child. *It is therefore necessary to understand what may inhibit parental responses to children and what the consequences of that inappropriate response may be for children of different ages.*
(Department of Health, 2000; our emphasis).

Discussion of parental disability throughout the document centres on the potential impact upon the disabled adult's parenting capacity and responses, to the exclusion of considering how best to tackle barriers to social inclusion and how best to address parental support needs, (Jones et al, 2002; Wates, 2002). This isolation of the 'parenting capacity' of disabled adults, as if it were a personal characteristic separable from environmental, social and organisational contexts, may have an effect that is counter to the integrative aims of the Framework.

In the Framework practice guidance there is extensive discussion of the impact of socio-economic factors such as housing, family social integration, employment, income and so on, in relation to disabled children. However, unresolved difficulties in these areas will have an equally substantial – in some cases even greater – impact on children's welfare where it is the parent rather than the child who has impairments. Yet neither the policy nor the practice guidance issued as part of the Framework direct the attention of assessors using it to family and environmental factors affecting families in which a disabled adult is present.

At the same time, the opportunity is missed to invite service providers to adopt a self-critical approach to elements in their own practice that might create or exacerbate difficulties experienced by families in which one or both parents are disabled, although there is encouragement to do this in relation to other groups of parents, such as those from minority ethnic communities (some of whom will of course also be disabled).

family and parenting support: the missing parents

The influence of an ecological perspective can be seen in a number of research studies looking at the effectiveness of family support and parenting education. What is striking in this developing literature, however, is the absence of disabled parents and any discussion of the access issues they face. For instance, in her review of issues in the establishment of parenting support and education classes, Smith (1997) talks about access issues in relation to a range of potentially marginalised groups, including fathers, parents from minority ethnic communities and people experiencing socio-economic disadvantage. However, no mention is made of access issues for disabled parents, except in relation to the importance of making sure that parents with learning difficulties can 'cope with the demands of the course'. Similarly, in her work on the impact of parent training programmes, Webster-Stratton (1999) points to the concentration hitherto on mothers at the expense of fathers, and to the difficulties parents from minority ethnic backgrounds can face. Once again, there is no mention of disabled parents. Other examples include the work of Roker and Coleman (1998) on programmes for parents of teenagers, which discusses access issues in terms of, among others, lone parents, parents of adopted children, parents in stepfamilies, parents of disabled children, gay and lesbian parents, parents who are travellers, and parents in rural areas. Again, the absence of disabled parents from this agenda is unfortunate.

This exclusion from the mainstream parent support literature is all the more a matter for concern given the evidence that disabled parents' access to antenatal education and parent support on the ground is very limited (particularly for parents with learning difficulties, Deaf parents and parents with visual impairments). Disabled parents have expressed concern that the lack of provision for them alongside other parents in the mainstream propels them to become users of social services in ways that they experience as isolating and stigmatising (Wates, 2003).

In a mapping exercise carried out in order to ascertain a picture of the development of parenting support nationally, the National Family and Parenting Institute (NFPI) found that only around one in five services said they had made specific efforts aimed at including disabled parents (Henricson et al, 2001). In addition, the survey highlighted the fact that apart from non-English speaking members of minority ethnic communities, disabled people featured highest in the list of those thought to face particular difficulties in accessing support schemes.

Clearly there is still a lot of work to be done in getting disabled parents onto mainstream parenting support agendas in relation to both research and practice. In 2002, the NFPI, in association with the Joseph Rowntree Foundation, commissioned a practice resource for professionals working with disabled parents (Olsen and Tyers, 2003). This willingness of mainstream parent support organisations to address the invisibility of disabled parents is to be welcomed, although some other recent work from the NFPI is not so inclusive. For instance, work on the information needs of parents (Henricson, 2002) does not discuss the information needs of disabled parents, and work concerning the relationship between parents and the state again leaves out issues for disabled parents, despite discussing the issues in relation to fathers, step-parents and those from minority ethnic communities (Henricson, 2003).

resilience

A growing body of literature over the past 10-15 years has examined factors that promote 'resilience' in individuals, families and communities under stress.

The literature on resilience is quite cohesive, in the sense that it tends to describe features associated with the person (which could be temperamental, biogenetic, behavioural), the family (parents and siblings) and the environment (extended family, neighbourhood, etc.) that promote positive outcomes in potentially adverse circumstances.

In terms of our categories, the literature spans personalised, ecological and structural perspectives in so far as researchers may look at a range of factors, from the characteristics of individuals that will make them more resilient, through economic and social factors and the characteristics of good support. However, that the literature owes its theoretical allegiance primarily to ecological theories is attested by the fact that many of the studies cited in the Framework also appear in the bibliography of a recent overview of 'resilience' (Newman, 2002).

Once again, the studies home in on the same groups of families, with a particular interest in parents who are mental health system users or who have drug and alcohol related issues. At the same time, it is a literature that challenges too rigid an interpretation of risk. Guldberg (2000) suggests an official tendency routinely to apply the principle 'If there are no obvious drawbacks, and it doesn't cost us much, why not do it?' to situations of risk where children are involved. However, the 'hidden' drawback is the lack of opportunities for children to learn coping mechanisms, the excessive fears of parents, and the pressure on statutory services to respond precipitously.

Newman suggests that from the perspective of welfare providers, placing the emphasis on 'resilience' rather than 'risk' is challenging. This is not simply a matter of professionals seeking to emphasise the importance of their territory and attract status and funding. Professionals are desperately well aware of the consequences whenever the failure of local authorities to identify and respond appropriately to risk results in a child being harmed.

Also inherently challenging to professionals is the finding that the supports identified by parents and children themselves as most effective are often those located in non-professional, community and extended family contexts.

> Any review of literature inevitably tends to focus on the strategies that are or could be adopted by professionals. However, when children themselves are asked what helped them 'succeed against the odds', the most frequently mentioned factors are help from members of their extended families, peers, neighbours or informal mentors, rather than the activities of paid professionals ... The transient involvement of professionals is unlikely to be a good exchange for a lifetime commitment from family, friends or kinfolk. In developing conscious strategies to promote children's resilience, we must be careful not to undervalue these non-professional sources, and more

importantly, ensure that our actions do not result in such naturally occurring sources of support being weakened. (Newman, 2002)

Consultations with disabled parents confirm that peer support, friends and family and community based networks are extremely highly valued (Olsen and Clarke, 2003; Wates, 2003). The flip side to Newman's comment above is that it would be a mistake to underestimate the central contribution of statutory services, especially as traditional networks of support become less accessible to many families for economic and demographic reasons.

Resilience is related to the availability of social capital and professionals therefore have an important potential role in strengthening social capital in deprived and dispersed communities. For example, if parents with learning difficulties did not suffer from chronically unstable housing, they would have more reliable access to long-term friendships and community based supports and could rely on professionals less.

A question is, how can mainstream health, social, education and family support services establish more effective partnerships that will enable them to work both in a more joined-up and supportive fashion with each other and at the same time in partnership with voluntary organisations and community supports?

The work on 'resilience' is at its strongest where it spans individual, ecological and organisational factors and explores the relationship between them. Over and over again, poverty and a lack of social supports show up as key negative determinants, while the presence of financial and informal supports enable families to thrive through all manner of challenging circumstances.

The concept of 'resilience' usefully reminds us that what is missing from the official canon of literature on parenting in general, and that concerned with disabled parents in particular, is a place for accounts of successful parenting undertaken by the majority of parents, disabled or otherwise, and the difference it makes when good supports are in place. Where disabled parents are helped to carry out their parenting roles, their resulting empowerment appears to be a protective factor for the children. For example, the majority of children of parents diagnosed with schizophrenia matured into competent adults, and the ones who did best had parents whose parenting roles had been upheld and supported (Bleuler, 1978).

Equally important omissions are the accounts of the everyday resilience of 'good enough' parenting and, indeed, the bottom line resilience of having the courage quite simply to tell how hard things really are without giving up on the attempt to make things better for our children and ourselves as parents (Wates and Jade, 1999). There is much evidence of all these kinds to draw on; much of it emanating from disabled parents themselves and, in some cases, from their grown up children. (Finger, 1990; Preston, 1995; Booth and Booth,

1998a; Mason, 1992; Wates, 1997; Sherer-Jacobson, 1999; Wates and Jade, 1999). This literature relates also to the discussion (in a later section of this review) of the importance of disabled parents' input into increasing understanding of what makes for better supports.

What lessons can be learnt from the literature relating to resilience? It points towards the need to:

- develop the literature around disabled parents to consider the experience of successful families
- re-examine service structures to see in what ways they could foster the characteristics of responsiveness, flexibility, reliability and supportiveness that characterise family and community supports.

'young carers'

An important strand of research activity since the early 1990s has been that around 'young carers'. Much of this has been carried out by the Young Carers Research Group (now operating within the Centre for Child and Family Research) at Loughborough University, beginning with small-scale qualitative studies of 'young carers' and their parents (Aldridge and Becker, 1993 and 1994), through surveys of the characteristics of those children identified as 'young carers' (Dearden and Becker, 1995; Becker et al, 1998), to a concern with particular groups of 'young carers', such as those whose parents have 'severe and enduring mental illness' (Aldridge and Becker, 2003) and a concern with a particular aspect of the 'young caring' experience, such as the transition to adulthood (Dearden and Becker, 2000). At the same time, we have seen the development of a strong set of responses from disabled writers and their allies questioning the appropriateness of constructing the children of disabled parents as a welfare category (Gradwell, 1992; Keith and Morris, 1996; Olsen and Parker, 1997; Stables and Smith, 1999; Wates 2001).

The understanding of 'young carers' was initially built around relatively small-scale studies involving interviews with young people (and in some cases their parents too) known to 'young carers' projects (Meredith, 1992; Bilsborrow, 1992; Frank, 1995). The information provided by these early studies of 'young carers' has been important in establishing key issues for subsequent research into children's involvement in caring roles within the family, including trying to pin down the numbers of 'young carers', the significance of gender (of parent and child), age and family structure (especially the number of parents in the household). For instance, in their survey of over 2,000 children receiving support from 'young carer' services, Dearden and Becker (1995) found that only slightly more girls than boys were 'young carers' (57 per cent as opposed to 43 per cent), and that over half of 'young carers' live in single-parent families.

As well as the work carried out at Loughborough, other studies have looked at particular aspects of the 'young caring' experience. Crabtree and Warner (1999) examine the issue of 'young carers' being bullied in school, for example, while Madge and colleagues (2000) look at the experience of pre-adolescent children. Some studies responded to the difficulty that some earlier studies faced in recruiting 'young carers' from minority ethnic communities (Bilsborrow, 1992) by looking specifically at this issue. Shah and Hatton (1999) interviewed 19 Asian 'young carers' and generated findings consistent with general 'young carer' studies – for instance, in pointing to the particular issues associated with having a parent who is a mental health service user, or young people's involvement in the administration of medicines. They also pointed to the likelihood that children in single-parent families were less likely to share caring tasks with others, an important theme running through this body of work. While this research is welcome, it is clear that more needs to be done to look at the experience of disabled parents from minority ethnic backgrounds and the particular challenges they face in preventing the involvement of children in tasks and roles inappropriate to their stage of life. An important addition to the literature is the study by Jones and colleagues (2002) carried out at the Bibini Centre, a family support project in Manchester providing support to black families where children have caring responsibilities. The authors argue that:

> It is unhelpful to argue about whether black families experience greater condemnation than disabled people's families. Many black people have to deal simultaneously with both racist and disablist misinterpretations of their parenting. There are examples of black people being condemned on the basis of fantasies about aspects of their family life. In addition, black young people's caring responsibilities in childcare, domestic work and interpreting may have more to do with black families' strategies for coping with poverty, exclusion from support services, services' failure to provide interpreters, poor housing, ill health and long working hours, than with cultural practices.
> (Jones et al, 2002)

This is especially important given the different assumptions that can be made by professionals about the nature of informal care giving in minority ethnic families.

Finally, another interesting, and seldom cited, strand of research around 'young caring' issues was carried out by Fox (1995 and 1998) into the way in which different professions within education conceptualised the issue of the absence from school of 'children with home responsibilities'. His work, involving interviews with teachers, educational welfare officers and other professionals, showed how the explanatory framework within which professionals understand the nature of the perceived problem has a significant bearing on the way in which policy and practice responses are developed. On the whole, teachers thought that parents needed to be informed about the importance of education for their children, educational welfare officers thought schools (and education more generally) should better accommodate the difficulties these families faced, and 'therapists' saw the problem in terms of deep-seated and complex emotional problems in the individuals and families concerned. This research illuminates how a concept like 'young caring' is a social and professional construct, and how policy and practice responses depend on the theoretical framework in which it is first constructed.

The application of the research evidence in relation to 'young carers' is shifting its focus. The relatively uncritical construction of a new welfare category has given way to a more conscious focus on family support and a more explicit awareness of the structural antecedents to children's involvement in caring. The creation of the Centre for Child and Family Research at the University of Loughborough embeds the issue of 'young caring' more firmly within the context of developing family supports, although, as the name of the new centre suggests, the child remains the primary service focus.

An important piece of empirical research in this more consciously holistic approach is the study of the transition to adulthood of 'young carers' (Dearden and Becker, 2000). In interviews with 60 'young carers', the authors reiterate many of the educational and social consequences of 'caring' for children as they grow up, and they once again highlight the particular difficulties that single-parent families face. The root causes of the problem are seen as extending beyond the characteristics of the parents themselves and there is greater emphasis on the role that poverty and the lack of more appropriate alternatives play in children becoming involved in excessive caring:

> It is the absence of family-focused, positive and supportive interventions by professionals, often combined with inadequate income, which cause the negative outcomes associated with caring by children and young people. (Dearden and Becker, 2000)

This shift of emphasis in the work of 'young carers' researchers is important, not only in allowing greater dialogue between researchers approaching the issue from what, in the past, appeared to be polarised positions, but also in allowing the development of future research agendas which do not descend into an artificial choice between children's and parents' rights and which can begin to explore some of the genuine complexities involved in looking at disability in relation to caring within families (Aldridge and Wates, 2003).

At the same time, researchers more critical of the 'young carers' research paradigm have also looked afresh at the issues around caring within families. A study by Olsen and Clarke (2003) concludes that a wider perspective on 'young caring' is required, one that accommodates how families themselves perceive the situation. In particular, they argue that a more sophisticated approach to understanding the place of caring within relationships should be developed rather than seeing it simply as the product of either parental impairment or service failure). They also provide interesting data on the complex ways in which children themselves actively negotiate caring roles; in some cases resisting whilst others risk over-investing in them (see also Newman and Wates, 2003). Olsen and Clarke provide evidence which suggests that the framework for understanding younger children's (i.e., those under the age of ten) involvement in both domestic work and emotional support for parents can be very complex, with many parents reporting having to 'fend off' and 'manage' their children's attempts to help. Importantly, Olsen and Clarke also found that children in single-parent families were more likely to be involved in 'caring' and domestic work activity, and that the nature of that activity (in terms of the responsibility that it involved, even where the workload was not particularly heavy) was often different in single-parent families.

Newman (2003) usefully summarises what the 'young carers' literature has established and where its assertions are thin. He also touches upon the debate around appropriate and inappropriate caring:

> We know that valued social roles undertaken by children - if recognised and rewarded - have the capacity to function as a protective factor, though this process will be weakened or reversed if the roles are excessive, or undertaken beyond a child's developmental capacity. (Newman, 2003)

The question remains: what about the future of 'young carers' research? We would argue that more recent debate between those with competing theoretical approaches and practice backgrounds has laid the foundations of a new approach to research in this area, albeit one in which the language to be employed is still very much a matter for debate. (Our ongoing disassociation with the term 'young carers' is indicated by its insertion in inverted commas through this review). This will involve research which looks at effective ways of preventing children's involvement in inappropriate roles, and involves looking at emerging practice and service provision for disabled parents with greater attention to the implications for choice and independence in the way in which assistance is provided. It will also involve attempts to integrate research and evidence about children's involvement in 'caring' with other debates and policy agendas, such as those around the paid employment of children and the division of families into those who are 'work-rich' and 'work-poor' (for example, see Mizen et al, 1999). This is important, because it will help get away from the assumption that children's involvement in domestic work is driven solely by the presence of impairment, rather than by a whole range of factors (including the relationship between housework and pocket money, the values attached to inculcating helpful behaviour in children, the availability of paid work for children) which are similarly important considerations in families with non-disabled parents.

It is clear, then, that analysis by researchers coming from a disabled parents' perspective on the one hand, and a 'young carers' perspective on the other, increasingly appear to reach similar conclusions in terms of how and why young people become involved in caring roles. Researchers and workers involved in voluntary and statutory services to 'young carers' argue that to end services to 'young carers' would not help to meet the needs of young people involved in inappropriate or excessive levels of caring, some of whom are involved in situations of immediate family difficulty (Aldridge and Becker, 2003). Disabled parents argue that the ongoing development of 'young carers' as a welfare construct institutionalises and thus to some extent perpetuates the very situation it seeks to address.

Significant investment has taken place over the last ten years in the 'young carers' service infrastructure, much of it originating in the children's support sector. We would argue that the research findings themselves indicate the need for the development of more effective parental support, in the interests of children and adults alike.

Some of the children's charities and carers' organisations that have funded 'young carers' projects over a number of years are beginning to ask whether the emphasis should be shifted towards a style of working that more clearly upholds the entitlement of disabled adults to support with their parenting role, regarding this as key to the welfare of children. This would not preclude a fast response to crisis situations nor would it prevent the development of effective peer support to young people, but it would aim to address the root of the problem and, as such, may be more effective in terms of preventing both the financial and social costs of family breakdown (Newman and Wates, 2003).

The 'young carers' research community (Becker et al, 1998) and the disabled parents' lobby both emphasise a rights' based perspective (Morris, 2003 forthcoming). This in itself raises interesting questions and dilemmas: are we talking about children's rights, adults' rights, or a family rights perspective? Are there conflicts of interest or should these rights be understood as being fundamentally compatible? Do different interest groups work selectively within the framework of children's rights as defined by the United Nations, with some stressing the right of children to be involved in decisions about their future while others point out that the State also has a responsibility for helping parents to carry out their roles effectively (articles 5 and 18)? Where do the right to privacy and family life outlined in the Human Rights Act (1998) sit with the right of the State to intervene? What is the relationship between minimising risk and taking interventions proportionate to risk? It helps to recognise that we are operating in politically and socially sensitive territory and that if there are potential conflicts of interest within families, there are also conflicts of interest at the level of local and national politics in relation to funding sources and service status. There are a number of encouraging signs that the exploration of these delicate issues is at least beginning.

in summary

An 'ecological' approach to parenting has:
- been the dominant theoretical force behind both policy and practice developments over the last 20 years, including the *Framework for the Assessment of Children in Need and their Families* as well as training resources such as *Crossing Bridges*
- attempted to address the broader social and economic environment in which parenting takes place
- been influential in driving a body of research focusing on the inherent risks to children implied by parental disability, especially regarding parenting and mental health
- influenced a growing body of research about the factors that promote or inhibit resilience
- increasingly influenced the thinking of those looking at 'young caring', where we have seen a gradual shift away from emotive accounts of the impacts of impairments on children's caring responsibilities and development, to a more broadly based discussion of caring, disability and family life in relation to external supports
- influenced a body of work on access to mainstream parenting support which, thus far, has failed to include disabled parents.

At the same time, the relative invisibility of disabled parents within both the research and service agendas of mainstream family and parenting support serves further to isolate understanding of disabled parents within the narrow, impairment-specific, personalised framework discussed earlier.

The large and varied body of work discussed in this section has important potential for including all parents in the support agenda, but requires a clearer focus on identifying and addressing the social origins of disablement and on the need for more decisive action to ensure that disabled parents have access to appropriate information and support. In the following sections of this review, we identify research perspectives that seek to move beyond the limitations of earlier research in this area.

organisational: an examination of structural contexts

There is a smaller body of work to discuss in this section but it is appropriate to go into rather more depth in discussing work that, in our opinion, provides evidence of a critical shift; with service providers and the voluntary sector recognising the need to examine elements of their own practice that may expedite or hinder the development of supportive practice in relation to disabled adults with parenting responsibilities.

A Jigsaw of Services

In 1997 a consortium of disabled parents and organisations involved in disability and family rights sought a meeting with inspectors from the Social Services Inspectorate (SSI). The consortium expressed its concern that unless the children of disabled adults were classified as 'children in need', 'at risk' or else 'young carers', parents seemed in many cases unable to obtain support. There was also concern about a number of cases in which disabled parents had lost custody of their children, either through child protection proceedings or in the divorce courts, without their support needs as disabled adults in relation to parenting ever having been assessed or addressed.

Parents felt that their support needs as parents fell between adult community care services and children and family teams, resulting in delays, failure to provide a service, or service approaches that undermined rather than assisted their parenting role. Many parents reported that they felt hesitant to approach social services for fear of attracting stigmatising labels to their families, or wary that their children might end up being removed from home.

In response to these expressions of concern, in 1999 and 2000 the SSI carried out an inspection in eight local authorities to examine what support was currently offered to disabled adults with their parenting role, and what could be done to improve services to this group of service users. The findings of the report, A Jigsaw of Services (Goodinge, 2000) bore out concerns that had been expressed by the consortium. Overall, the inspectors found little evidence of a co-ordinated service response either within social services departments or between relevant local authority and other agencies. In addition, according to the inspectors' own analysis of casework records involving disabled parents, family needs were being met by service provision in only 30 per cent of the records examined in detail .

The SSI inspection is the largest survey to date of disabled parents' experiences of services, involving, as it does, several hundred parents once interviews, consultations and record analysis are included. As such, it marks a considerable step forward. For the first time, it provides evidence from a government source of the difficulties facing disabled parents as a distinct group of users in accessing services. It sets out a number of recommendations for more explicit and better co-ordinated practice in respect of disabled adults with parenting responsibilities.

The prevalence of parents with learning difficulties whose children become involved in child protection procedures was not felt by the inspectors to be justified by the casework describing what was happening in those families. The inspectors suggest these high numbers may stem, at least in part, from the way in which services respond to certain groups of parents, the omission of parenting tasks and responsibilities from eligibility criteria for community care services, and the reluctance in some areas to recognise disabled adults' additional needs as parents (Goodinge, 2000).

supporting disabled adults in their parenting role

Following the publication of *A Jigsaw of Services*, the Joseph Rowntree Foundation (JRF) commissioned research to inform an inter-agency Task Force aimed at improving service provision to disabled parents. Social services departments were asked to provide examples of protocols and policies used in relation to supporting parents with physical and sensory impairments, and parents with learning difficulties.

Many of these were protocols formalising arrangements for working across adults' and children and family divisions. However, a detailed study of the policies and protocols revealed tensions not only at the level of co-ordinating structures, records, budgets, training, and so on, but, more fundamentally, between operational understandings of the two sets of legislation involved (specifically, the Children Act 1989 and legislation policy and practice guidance concerning disabled adults) in relation to each other. The report concluded that neither is being used to ensure that disabled adults' entitlement to support in fulfilling their parenting responsibilities is addressed as a matter of course by local authorities. In particular, services to disabled adults are seen as being restricted to meeting the personal care needs of the disabled individual. Social services departments have not generally interpreted this as including the adult's needs in respect of parenting tasks and roles. However this omission is challenged by the *Fair Access to Care Services Guidance* issued by the Department of Health in 2002 (Department of Health, 2002b), which states that parenting is included in the social roles that should be considered as part of an assessment of a disabled adult's needs (see Appendix).

Whether the appropriate need is being assessed and addressed, under which legislation and at what point this happens, all depend upon the extent to which, and the manner in which, information is shared between divisions and agencies. The SSI inspectors found that in many places adult services teams fail to record routinely that there are children in the family, whereas children's services teams fail to record routinely the presence of a disabled parent (Goodinge, 2000). Although the policies and protocols say that information should be shared across divisions, few departments appear to have established systematic mechanisms for such cross-referencing at an early stage with a view to preventing problems from arising in families.

Although social services departments are aware that disabled adults are wary of approaching social services for support with parenting, few measures are taken to allay these fears and there is generally little evidence that departments are designing services in a way that would lessen anxieties and/or increase access:

> Social services departments' consultations with disabled parents highlighted
> that the concerns uppermost in the minds of disabled parents as they
> approach social services departments - anxieties that social services will be
> critical of their parenting, concerns about ongoing scrutiny and fear of
> stigmatising labels being applied to their families - may be quite different
> from the concerns uppermost in the minds of service providers as they
> prepare policies or protocols. (Wates, 2002)

The JRF process evaluation also identified that the continuation of appropriate specialist adult support, although clearly crucial to effective communications with parents experiencing difficulties, may very easily fall away from the agenda when there are child protection concerns.

Disabled parents are deterred from seeking potentially valuable support by a perception that social services departments are predominantly concerned with child protection issues and have nothing to offer them by way of support with parenting, or will intervene in ways that undermine rather than support them in their parenting role. Furthermore, anxieties are expressed about potentially conflicting roles held by social services departments in relation to parents and there was concern at the possibility that what appeared to be temporary relief offered to families experiencing difficulties, might result in children becoming 'looked after' on a longer term basis (Wates, 2002).

parents with learning difficulties

The last decade has seen the development of an influential body of research into the experiences of parents with learning difficulties carried out by Tim and Wendy Booth at the University of Sheffield (Booth and Booth, 1993a and b, 1994a and b, 1998a and b). Some of this work involves interviews and other innovative methods appropriate for the inclusion of people with learning difficulties (including narrative story methods and drawings) with parents themselves, as well as with children having grown up with parents with learning difficulties.

Booth and Booth provide evidence that the parenting difficulties encountered by these parents are similar to those experienced by other non-disabled parents living in poor economic circumstances:

> Experiences [of parents with learning difficulties] of parenthood and child-
> rearing show more similarities than differences with other ordinary families
> from the same social background. (Booth and Booth, 1993a)

They also point to the importance of key people within the social support network of parents with learning difficulties in reducing the isolation those parents experience (Booth and Booth, 1994b). In addition, Booth and Booth demonstrate how poor IQ is often used as a proxy for the quality of parenting provided, and argue against a 'presumption of neglect' based on artificial, medicalised measures of intelligence (Booth and Booth, 1994b). Furthermore, they provide case studies that demonstrate the critical importance of professional judgement, either in supporting parents with learning difficulties or in undermining them (Booth and Booth, 1993b).

The practice implications from this body of research are focused on reducing and mediating the impact of broader forms of disadvantage on parenting skills and on a recognition that parenting skills develop and change over time and that abilities in parenting can be nurtured and encouraged with appropriate support. This is also the basis of the Cornwall Special Parenting Service and its offshoot Open Doors, which combines advice and support about parenting with employment skills and other training opportunities, and it is also the basis of the research work informing these service developments (McGaw, 1995 and 2000).

Recent work on the parenting of people with learning difficulties raises similar points about the importance of the presence or absence of support in influencing outcomes, and about the disadvantages faced by these parents within court proceedings. McConnell and colleagues (2002) looked at 285 court cases brought by child protection agencies in Sydney, Australia, which featured parents with learning difficulties. They found that negative beliefs about parental capacity, an adversarial legal system that acted as a barrier to effective legal representation on the part of parents, and an absence of supportive services, all contributed to the higher level of separation from their children experienced by these parents. Work by Feldman and colleagues (2002) has shown how mothers with learning difficulties experience high levels of stress and social isolation, pointing to the importance of helping to maintain strong informal networks of support. Similarly, a study comparing learning and behavioural outcomes for 27 school-age children of economically poor mothers with learning difficulties compared to 25 controls (living in similar economic circumstances but without disabled mothers), found that intellectual impairment did have an effect which was not explained solely by poverty (Feldman and Walton-Allen, 1997). However, the authors also point to the fact that maternal social supports were less available to mothers with learning difficulties, emphasising again the importance of support to this group of parents.

Several studies in this area have pointed to the way in which the parenting of people with learning difficulties is judged by different standards, and with less 'leeway', than for the population as a whole. For instance, Andron and Tymchuk (1987) provide evidence that the use of minor forms of physical punishment are cited more decisively by the authorities as evidence of parenting failure in relation to parents with learning difficulties than for other parents, a point supported by Campion in relation to disabled parents generally:

> Middle class parents are not subject to the same sort of scrutiny as those
> from poor backgrounds...This is perhaps an indication that professionals find
> surveillance of groups that they see as different easier to carry out – it is
> much more uncomfortable to scrutinise your own kind in the same way.
> (Campion, 1995)

In a similar way, parents with learning difficulties can find their response to inaccessible information about school events, for example, interpreted as saying something about their (lack of) commitment to their children's education, when in fact the problem lies in the inaccessible way in which information is presented.

Valuing People

There is growing recognition in central government policies and priorities of the entitlement of people with learning difficulties to assistance in respect of their family and social roles and responsibilities. The government White Paper, Valuing People: A New Strategy for Learning Disability for the 21st Century, stressed the necessity for 'children and adult service teams to work closely together to develop a common approach' (Department of Health, 2001). Sub-objective 7.3 of the White Paper reads as follows:

> Supporting people with learning disabilities in order to help them, wherever
> possible, ensure their children gain maximum life chance benefits.
> (Department of Health, 2001)

The findings of the SSI inspection (Goodinge, 2000) underlined that the issue of sustaining support for parents where there are concerns for child welfare is particularly crucial in relation to parents with learning difficulties. For these parents, as for others, research has shown that specialist support and advocacy services are often key to long-term outcomes within families (Booth and Booth, 1998b).

The concerns expressed in A Jigsaw of Services, accounts given by parents with learning difficulties at a day seminar organised by the Department of Health in June 2000 and reported in DPPi Journal (DPPi, 2001), and related research findings (Booth and Booth, 1998b; McGaw, 2000) all contributed to the preparation of the White Paper:

> People with learning disabilities can be good parents and provide their
> children with a good start in life, but may require considerable help to do so.
> This requires children and adult social services teams to work closely
> together to develop a common approach. Social services departments have a
> duty to safeguard the welfare of children, and in some circumstances a
> parent with learning disabilities will not be able to meet their child's needs.
> However, we believe this should not be the result of agencies not arranging
> for appropriate and timely support. (Department of Health, 2001)

In spite of this promising development, it is of concern that various Department of Health initiatives arising out of the Valuing People initiative fail to mention that adults with learning difficulties may also have parenting responsibilities. The following omissions are noted in the final report of the Joseph Rowntree Foundation Task Force on support for disabled adults with parenting responsibilities (Morris, 2003):

- maternity services are not mentioned in the good practice guidance on health action plans
- support to parents with learning difficulties is not mentioned in the guidance for Learning Disability Partnership Boards on implementing Person Centred Planning
- parenting is not mentioned at all in the guidance on Person Centred Planning.

supporting parents with mental health, alcohol or drug problems

A body of work looking at the importance of organisational and service issues in relation to the parenting of mental health service users is also beginning to develop. Hawes and Cottrell (1999) looked at 51 mothers admitted to psychiatric hospital in the UK, and found that a significant number of their children had to move home as a result, with children of single mothers particularly affected. In a study of the records of 13 mothers experiencing severe mental distress whose children were the subject of child protection proceedings, Stanley and Penhale (1999) found that in nine cases no adult mental health social worker was involved, with no community psychiatric nurse involvement in seven of the cases.

Coleman and Cassell (1994) gathered information on 95 consecutively admitted patients in a UK psychiatric hospital, and found that those who were parents experienced additional anxieties about arrangements for their children's care. The authors make the important point that mental health impairments and child care concerns can act reciprocally – in other words, that anxiety about arrangements for children can adversely affect mental health, which in turn can lead to longer periods of admission and, therefore, additional concerns about child care. Of course, anxieties about arrangements for children can also act as a barrier to people seeking mental health service support in the first place.

An Oxfordshire-based study of cross divisional work and joint agency working to support parents with mental health or substance misuse problems and their dependent children, found that examples of good innovative and responsive service provision exist but 'tend not to be formalised or embedded within any organisation' (Partridge, 2001).

Although the recent study by Aldridge and Becker (2003), in common with other work from the Centre for Child and Family Research, is concerned with impacts upon 'young carers' first and foremost, the authors examine the 'negative associations' of professionals in relation to parental mental health, resulting in inappropriate professional responses and the counter-productive nature of some inter-agency responses.

In 1999, researchers based at the National Institute for Social Work (NISW) were commissioned by the Department of Health to carry out a research and development project looking 'at the interfaces within and between services for families where a parent has a persistent mental health, alcohol or drug problem'. This work, which is still ongoing although now under the auspices of the Social Care Institute for Excellence (SCIE), began by examining policies and protocols in use by social services departments and by talking with senior officers and frontline practitioners in local authorities' children's services about the operation of services to these groups of parents and their families (Kearney et al, 2000).

The second phase of this work has been to devise a template to guide the development of collaborative work between and with agencies and families, based on the details of good working practice provided by local authorities and in Department of Health policy documents. The group identify a shift in their own perception of this work as the links between different groups of parents became more apparent.

> During the course of this project we have noted a radical shift in thinking which will have a major positive effect on the problems that these protocols aim to solve. The catalyst for this change in thinking has come from the user-led definition of 'disabled parents', which includes parents with mental health, drug and alcohol problems. (Kearney et al, 2003)

Sayce (1999) has written about the importance of recognising the equal opportunities of parents who are mental health service users, and argues that a 'civil rights' approach is necessary in order to address the barriers faced by this group of parents.

relationships with professionals

Olsen and Clarke (2003) interviewed disabled parents and family members in 80 families. As well as identifying the range of barriers to accessing support that disabled parents can face, they also highlighted the important role that professionals can play both in undermining and underpinning parenting roles. Several parents pointed to key moments when health or social care professionals effectively closed doors to support, for instance by saying that non-disabled partners should give up work to become full-time carers, without looking for alternative ways in which disabled parents could be provided with support. On the other hand, some disabled parents pointed to extremely effective support they had received, often involving an alliance between the family and key professionals, such as a GP or advocate, in levering greater formal support from agencies such as social services departments.

Wates (2003) also found a mixed picture in terms of disabled parents' perceptions of professional support. Any one of a range of professionals, including family doctors, midwives, health visitors, occupational therapists, social workers or teachers, may be picked out by one parent as having given excellent information, moral support and useful referrals to other sources of help, while another parent will mention the same professional group as having been unhelpful. A number of parents indicated that their experience had varied from one encounter to another within the same professional group. However, alongside a general picture of support characterised by its patchiness, distinct patterns of response emerged in relation to different professional groups (Wates, 2003).

Many parents are hesitant to approach social services in case this is seen as a sign that they are having difficulties. The process of assessment, especially when this is done in the context of 'children in need', is felt by many to raise questions about their capacities as parents. Sources of information and support (including specialist supports) accessed through primary health care and mainstream avenues of parent and family support are generally more acceptable to parents precisely because they are keyed in with the services that all parents use.

The consultation findings underline the need to make professionals and organisations in the family and parent support sector (whether governmental or non-governmental) more aware of their legal obligation under the 1995 Disability Discrimination Act to meet the support and information needs and service entitlements of disabled parents. This is in line with a growing awareness in the voluntary and statutory sectors of the need to be proactive in promoting social inclusion.

The findings also underscore the need to develop joined-up work across agencies, facilitating 'points of entry' to both mainstream and specialist services. A further important finding was the extreme difficulty many parents experience in finding information and support when family needs change suddenly. Systems that do not have the flexibility to respond quickly and appropriately at such times can have a negative impact by prolonging and exacerbating difficulties that families experience.

in summary

The pieces of work discussed in this section are important because they move beyond a concern with individual failings to take into account the organisational and service-related barriers that parents may encounter. For instance, Olsen and Clarke (2003) discuss the importance of other forms of structural exclusion, based on socio-economic disadvantage, gender, racism and so on, in structuring the experience of disabled parents.

This section has looked at a variety of research studies and other papers, which have suggested the following:

- to understand the origin of difficulties faced by disabled parents and their families, it is important to look at the structural and economic contexts within which parenting takes place
- when appropriate supports (formal and informal) are available, it may make a critical difference for the better to parenting outcomes
- inadequate service responses can act as barriers to the provision of effective and timely support.

This body of work has identified that parenting by disabled people cannot be understood simply in terms of identifying individual attributes and capacities only with a view to assessing the potential 'risk' to child welfare that different groups of parents represent. Rather, the parenting of disabled people, along with that of parents in the wider population, should be as well supported as possible. The level of support that parents have access to can be severely hampered or else significantly facilitated by organisational, physical, economic and attitudinal considerations.

In the next section, we look at the characteristics of research on disabled parents based in a social model understanding of disability. We examine some of the methodological considerations involved in making sure that those who stand to be most affected by the results of research are fully represented within the research process.

new directions

In this section we look at the emergence of a body of research relating to disabled parents that is informed by the Social Model of Disability in which the observations, insights and participation of disabled parents are seen as key to developing a research and policy agenda aimed at identifying and removing barriers and fostering better support to disabled people and their families.

increasing the status of 'user' knowledge

As has been shown, a great deal of the research with a bearing on the lives of disabled parents starts out from the assumption that disability is an individual characteristic (whether physical, sensory, cognitive, or related to mental health) that can be expected to have a negative impact on parenting. We suggest that research consistent with the social model of disability directs attention to the social and economic contexts within which family life takes place. Attitudes towards disabled people who become parents, their access to facilities and resources and the way in which services are planned and delivered all have a more far-reaching impact upon parenting than impairment in and of itself. (Finkelstein, 1992; Oliver, 1992)

There is already in existence a great deal of knowledge, information and insight supplied by disabled parents themselves. See for example, Finger, 1990; Keith, 1994; Mason, 1992; Morris, 1992; Shackle, 1993; Sherer-Jacobson, 1999; Wates and Jade, 1999; and a wide range of first hand accounts in Disability, Pregnancy and Parenthood international journal from 1993 to the present.

However, personal accounts, user feedback and service provider concerns are generally regarded as less authoritative than work by paid academics. In part it may be that information from a 'user' perspective tends to be less effectively disseminated, but there may also be doubts about its status as knowledge. As a result much valuable information has tended to be overlooked by the research community and by policy makers, a point acknowledged by Pawson and colleagues (2003) in introducing a report commissioned by the Social Care Institute for Excellence (SCIE) on types and quality of social care knowledge:

> It is important not to neglect sources of knowledge that are tacit, that currently lack prestige and seem less compelling, (Pawson et al, 2003)

A number of recent academic studies, current research and journal articles by researchers (many of whom are themselves disabled people) are helping to fill specific gaps in the information available. Examples include work on Deaf parents' experience of maternity services (Tracey, 2002; Chowdry, 2002; Iqbal, 2004; Weiner, 2002), mental health and parenting (Olkin, 1999; Doe, 2002; Sikand, 2002), disabled lesbian mothers (O'Toole and D'aoust, 2000), sexuality, disability and reproductive rights (Parens and Asch, 2000; Block et al,

2002) parents with learning difficulties (DPPi, 2001; BILD, 2000 and 2002), the experience of black disabled parents (Bignall et al, 2001; Jones et al, 2002) disabled parents' access to adaptive equipment (Ricability, 2000; Vensand et al, 2000) and communications with children's schools (Robinson et al, 2001; Bullivant and DPPi editorial team, 2001). In addition, a number of researchers have provided overviews of disabled adults' experience in relation to disability and parenting in the UK, US and elsewhere (Keith and Morris, 1996; Toms-Barker and Maralani, 1997; Block, 2002; Wates, 1997 and 2003).

It is imperative to place these perspectives before policymakers and service providers in the statutory and voluntary sectors and thought should therefore be given to raising the profile and prestige of writing and research on disabled parents informed by a social model perspective.

creating appropriate methodologies

There are a great many unanswered and partially answered questions at this point about what the research should be addressing, what the most effective and appropriate methodologies are, the power relations between researchers and participants and the involvement of disabled parents in the dissemination and application of research that has the potential to make their lives both easier and more difficult (Bailey, 2003; Barnes, 2003; Mercer, 2002).

This debate is not without ironies. There is, for example, an inherent question as to the representative-ness of research based in a participatory model. A major limitation is that groups from which participants are drawn tend to be limited. The families involved in 'young carers' research, for example, have overwhelmingly been young people known to 'young carers' projects and their parents. It is not surprising therefore that parents interviewed in 'young carers' research consistently report that they find such projects valuable and feel there is a need to develop services to 'young carers'. The majority of disabled parents, who are not involved in these projects, would not necessarily share this view.

By the same token, all the parents who participated in the recent consultation by Disabled Parents Network (Wates, 2003) were members of local or national networks with a peer support focus. It was not surprising that these parents, whilst keen to have access to family and parenting activities and information, were very positive about the value of support networks and local groups of disabled parents. However when the same researcher interviewed a group of disabled parents not linked to support organisations (Wates, 1997), a number of them were keen to distance themselves from groups or networks that they saw as linked with disability and thus, in their view, outside the mainstream of parent and family support.

This does not make what is learnt from self-selected research participants any less important. But it does raise the fundamental question of what have been described as 'the silenced voices' (Corker 1999); for implicit in the idea of participants is the idea of non-participants. What of the disabled parents who have declined to be involved in either the support groups or the research projects, and what about those whom nobody has approached to speak about their experience in relation to meeting their children's needs? What do they think of the supports available to them?

Participatory research necessarily implies a willingness to be involved on the part of those whose situation is being examined, but beyond this, and not always addressed, is the question of how research findings will be interpreted and the use to which they will be put. Even where there is a degree of ownership of the research process, it cannot be assumed from this that participants will be interested in, or have access to, the output (which often takes the form of a densely written report). Nor is there necessarily any prior agreement about the extent to which disabled parents involved as research participants will also be involved in analysis and dissemination or have control over any policy conclusions arrived at as a result of the research (Bailey, 2003).

Researchers and social theorists rightly look for qualities of trustworthiness and transparency in research. However agreement within a particular research community that a piece of work is 'trustworthy' may say more about the values shared by members of that particular community than it does about the elusive notion of verifiable truth. Another community may regard the same piece of work with deep suspicion. As Geoff Mercer of the Centre for Disability Studies at Leeds University points out:

> The application of formal tests of 'quality control' promoted by mainstream research rarely allows for the specific circumstances of research with disabled (Sample, 1996; Stalker, 1998).
> (Barnes and Mercer [eds], 2003)

There is no reason why large-scale quantitative studies involving large, randomised surveys of disabled parents with a control group drawn from the population of non-disabled parents should not be compatible with the social model of disability; increasing understanding of the barriers faced by disabled parents and their families and directed towards improving the support available.

Indeed, it might be useful to combine the strengths of qualitative and quantitative approaches, for example beginning from personal accounts with loosely structured interviews and proceeding to examine questions that have emerged as key in initial analysis with larger samples representative of the study population.

areas where knowledge is needed

A recent consultation with over 150 disabled parents commissioned by the Disabled Parents Network and funded by the Department of Health (Wates, 2003) indicated a number of areas where further investigation is needed in relation to disabled parents. These included: finding ways to key parents more effectively into mainstream health services and family support, co-ordinating routine and crisis access to specialist health and social services, meeting disabled parents needs within hospitals, outcomes for parents who make complaints, and access to advocacy and legal services. It will be timely and useful to look at the application of the Disability Discrimination Act 1995, further sections of which are due for implementation by 2004, to the provision of services, goods and information; including schools' communications with disabled parents.

Given the increasingly well-established link between poverty and households that contain disabled members and more particularly disabled adults (Department of Work and Pensions, 2001; Gordon et al, 2000), the economic situation of families must be a key factor in analysis of the situation of disabled parents.

We would like to highlight the need for investigative collaboration involving disabled parents and service providers from a range of relevant agencies; examining more closely some of the areas of difficulty that have been identified. (Wates, 2003; Olsen and Tyers, 2003)

Olsen and Tyers have made a start on this. Their sobering observation however, confirming the impressions of Goodinge (2000) and Wates (2002), is that there is still at this stage very little joined-up working directed at support for disabled adults in their parenting role. Rather, it appears that pockets of interesting and innovative practice are emerging (often dependent on the determination of key individuals) that rarely extend beyond the confines of particular teams or divisions within an organisation.

creating a forum for research and development

There are considerable and as yet unanswered questions about developing support to disabled parents at local level across statutory services, non-governmental organisations and informal community supports. Now is a time of opportunity with many initiatives having the potential to develop the social inclusion agenda in relation to disabled adults and their children: Early Years, Sure Start, Community Safety, Drug Action Teams, Neighbourhood Renewal, Local Neighbourhood Partnerships, Health Action Zones, Primary Care Trusts, Partnership Boards, The Children's Fund, Local Prevention Strategies, Information and Referral Tracking and Children's Trusts, to mention a few. However the plethora of initiatives, each with different structures, different personnel, overlapping agendas and distinct yet often competing funding streams, is also a potential difficulty. Many of the initiatives mentioned above are targeted at deprived areas, or particular sections of the population, making it hard to see how they can be used systematically to assist the access of disabled parents to mainstream services.

In addition, the increasing separation of services to children (including the children of disabled parents) and disabled adults (including disabled adults with parenting responsibilities for dependant children) makes it potentially even harder than before to co-ordinate genuinely holistic provision for families. It would be all too easy for disabled parents to go on falling through the gaps.

Disabled parents have a key role in establishing the questions that research should be addressing, managing and monitoring the quality of research and, where appropriate, in carrying it out and following through on the way in which findings are shared and taken up.

The Nuffield Community Care Studies Unit at the University of Leicester has organised a series of seminars funded by the Economic and Social Research Council looking at policy, practice and research developments concerned with the development of supports to disabled parents (2002-2004). One seminar in the series will focus specifically on disseminating the growing body of research carried out by disabled parents themselves. A number of the researchers concerned propose setting up an informal research forum centred on the issue of disabled parents and working explicitly to the social model of disability that will seek to fulfil the following aims:

- to raise the profile and prestige of this body of research, influence policy and practice and thereby improve the situation of disabled parents and their families
- establish the central role of disabled parents themselves in developing research questions, devising methodologies fit for purpose, carrying out, evaluating and disseminating research
- build up a representative picture of disabled parents, including voices that have been largely missing from the debate up to this point
- attract the partnership and participation of academic institutions and potential funding bodies to identify research needs in this area and ensure that these studies are designed and carried out with sufficient rigour, whilst using appropriate methodologies and accessible means
- work on more effective filing, referencing and dissemination of findings, avoiding unnecessary duplication and helping to draw out the links between related pieces of work
- decrease the potential isolation of researchers and research participants working outside formal academic contexts
- promote participatory and emancipatory models of research as a body of work with identifiable characteristics, in terms of methodology, management and dissemination.

conclusions

disabled adults with parenting responsibilities: supportive intentions – supportive practice

There is both a legal and a moral imperative to uphold the welfare of children by seeking to ensure that all parents – including those with physical and sensory impairments, learning difficulties, users of the mental health system, parents with drug and alcohol issues, Deaf parents, and disabled parents from black and minority ethnic communities – receive appropriate and timely support. In this review we have tried to show how much of the research that has been carried out in this area has not been concerned with social context or with support, but has homed in on disabled parents as an area of parenting pathology.

We have shown how, as researchers' attention has increasingly been directed towards parenting within broader social and economic contexts, this is only gradually being applied consistently to disabled parents as to others. Since the publication of A Jigsaw of Services, more attention has been given to the way in which services are organised and delivered and how this may, in itself, impact on parenting.

We have discussed the key role of parents and their families in identifying what we need to know, ensuring that the information that is gathered is representative of disabled parents in the ordinary population, that it is as far as possible inclusive of until now missing voices, and that findings are used to bring about improvements in support to disabled adults in their parenting role.

In spite of the supportive intentions and potential within both community care legislation and the Children Act 1989, the assumption that parental disability will, to a greater or lesser extent, negatively impact on children has resulted in a research focus on parenting capacity and child protection rather than examining wider issues of socio-economic contexts and addressing parent support issues. This in turn has resulted in the delivery of services that disabled parents frequently perceive as undermining, rather than supporting them in their parenting role.

At the same time, the failure to include disabled adults in either the research or service agenda of mainstream parent and family support organisations and health support networks, and the strong association between disability and family poverty, increase the likelihood of the (anticipated) difficulties occurring within families. In reality, disabled parents are no different from others. They do better with support and their parenting is adversely affected by poverty, social exclusion and systematic disadvantage.

The right to privacy and respect for family life set out in the Human Rights Act 1998, and the requirement of the 1995 Disability Discrimination Act 'that service providers have to take reasonable steps to change policies, practices or procedures which make it impossible or unreasonably difficult for disabled people to use a service', are compatible with children's rights and the duty of the state (through local authorities) to safeguard and promote the welfare of children.

There is still much work to be done to establish support for disabled parents as part of ongoing research and policy and practice agendas. It is essential to build on the momentum of recent initiatives, such as the series of ESRC-funded seminars and the emergence of an informal research forum, both of which look at disabled parents as a distinctive research priority informed by the social model of disability; the emergence of research and practice development seminars involving local authorities; the work of the JRF Task Force (Morris, 2003); and consultations with disabled parents (Wates, 2003; Olsen and Tyers, 2003). In addition, more effective support will only happen to the extent that disabled parents' issues are routinely and systematically included in the training of professionals, and continuous professional development at local and national level.

disabled adults with parenting responsibilities: a checklist for good practice

The purpose of this review is to promote research that will result in more effective support to disabled parents and their children. It seems good, therefore, to end with a checklist of questions (adapted and extended from Wates, 2002) that local authorities and other relevant agencies may find useful as a basis for enquiring into existing practices in their own area.

1   Are disabled adults (including parents with physical and sensory impairments, Deaf parents, parents with learning difficulties, those who are users of mental health system and those with drugs and alcohol issues) recognised as service users with support needs in relation to parenting?
2   Is there clear agreement about how Community Care legislation, in combination with children's legislation where appropriate, is to be used to support disabled parents and families?
3   Where policies/protocols/procedures exist, are they in use and are all staff and relevant bodies aware of what they say?
4   Are parenting tasks and responsibilities included in eligibility criteria and covered in assessment procedures for adult services and benefits?
5   Is the meeting of needs associated with parenting responsibilities regarded as a priority for access to assessment and service allocation?
6   Are mechanisms in place that ensure timely and effective cross-referencing between different agencies and across

organisational divisions to ensure that disabled adults with parenting responsibilities are effectively keyed in to mainstream and specialist supports?

7   Do support systems have the flexibility and responsiveness to respond quickly and appropriately to changing family needs?

8   Do policies and protocols ensure that no disabled parents should be obliged to rely upon a family member for inappropriate levels of assistance or for help with inappropriate tasks?

9   Do policies and protocols make it clear that the children of disabled parents are not automatically regarded as vulnerable?

10 Can disabled adults access the parenting support they need without their children first having to be 'children in need' or 'young carers'?

11 In cases where there are child protection concerns, how is the ongoing involvement of both children's and adult specialist workers guaranteed and co-ordinated?

12 Do all parents have access to advocacy services?

13 Are cases in which child protection measures are taken, monitored to make sure that this is the most appropriate response?

14 Does the local authority record how many children whose parents are disabled are in long-term foster care, or in line for adoption?

15 Do agencies have procedures and staff appointed to support the development of joint working and inter-agency training across relevant statutory agencies and voluntary bodies?

16 Are clear arrangements in place across divisions of social services departments and between agencies for pooling budgets and sharing costs, where appropriate?

17 Might charging policies for parenting tasks be waived in line with a preventative approach to family support, regardless of which budget the support is funded from?

18 Are direct payments promoted to meet parenting support needs? Since this is possible both under Community Care legislation and under the Children Act 1989, are there arrangements for joint direct payments packages (which might also include health services) to be made where appropriate?

19 How many parents are receiving direct payments to assist them in their parenting role?

20 Are disabled parents consulted on their access to, and experience of, services intended to support them in their parenting role?

21 Is service information provided to disabled parents that explains what services they are entitled to and how to go about getting hold of them?

22 Is any service user information provided to disabled parents appropriate and accessible to parents from minority ethnic communities, parents with learning difficulties and Deaf parents, as well as to disabled parents generally?

23 Do agencies regularly monitor their practice, procedures and communication with disabled parents, to determine whether these are consistent with their supportive intentions?

24 Do disabled parents have full access to (including access to information about) local maternity services, primary health care, parent education and family facilities, including shops, sports, leisure, playgrounds, playgroups, schools etc.?

25 Do disabled parents have full access to (including access to information about) supports and volunteering opportunities for parents and families in the voluntary sector?

26 Are disabled parents' perceptions of services and agencies evaluated?

27 What steps have been taken to allay disabled parents' fears in relation to approaching service providers and to ensure that services are welcoming?

28 Are disabled parents involved in the development, monitoring and evaluation of services?

The list is necessarily long because it is intended to prompt reflection across a range of agencies and services. Readers may like to start by highlighting those questions of most immediate relevance and considering alongside which other agencies, groups and bodies the remaining questions might need to be addressed.

appendix

supporting disabled adults in their parenting role:
the legislative, policy and practice context

(adapted from a survey of social services policies and protocols in relation to disabled parents for the Joseph Rowntree Foundation by Michele Wates, April 2002)

the Children Act 1989

It is the clear intention of the Children Act 1989 both that specific support needs of disabled adults in relation to parenting should be addressed and also that service providers should seek, 'to promote and strengthen family ties and to deliver services in partnership with families'. Part III of the Children Act 1989 allows for the provision of services to parents to safeguard the welfare of children as far as possible within their own families. Paragraph 2.5 of the accompanying Regulations and Guidance is particularly relevant for children whose parents may be ill or disabled. This paragraph includes the following:

> Children should not necessarily be identified as in need because one or both parents is disabled, although this could of course be a factor. It may be that the provision of services to the parent, *either under adult disabled persons legislation or under 17(3) of the Act* may safeguard the welfare of the child sufficiently to enable the parent to continue looking after him at home. (The Children Act 1989, added emphasis)

This intention was further clarified in a letter from the Chief Inspector to directors of social services departments:

> Where the disabled person is a parent, it is essential that the community care assessment focuses on the family and considers how to support the parent and support the needs of any young carers. (Department of Health, 1995)

relevance of Community Care legislation to disabled parents

There is an array of adult and community care legislation that upholds disabled adults' entitlements to receive services appropriate to their individual needs. Where the disabled person has parenting responsibilities various statutes and governmental Guidance have implications for disabled parents' entitlements. These include the right to a needs led assessment in which all needs relevant to the individual are considered, including social and family roles, the right to see records and to be consulted, access to advocacy and personal support and the right to reasonable adjustments to service provision to ensure that it is available on the same terms to disabled as to non-disabled people.

new developments in legislation and guidance

In the past couple of years, following the publication of an SSI report and the efforts from a wide-ranging organisational base to improve services to disabled parents (Morris, 2003), amendments to legislation and guidance with a more direct bearing on meeting the needs of disabled parents have been introduced.

making direct payments for assistance with parenting tasks and responsibilities

The Community Care (Direct Payments) Act 1996 made it possible for social services departments to provide direct payments in lieu of services, to meet assessed needs. This could potentially include those relating to parenting. The Health and Social Care Act 2001 (which came into force in 2002) requires councils to make a direct payment to anyone who has been assessed as needing services, who requests one, and who is able to manage a direct payment, with assistance if necessary.

The Health and Social Care Act 2001 will also allow disabled parents to access direct payments to purchase services provided under the Children Act 1989, via an amended section 17a. This enables adult disability services, with input from children's and/or health services as and where appropriate, to put together a support package involving direct payments to support parenting and thereby safeguard the welfare of children. This should not automatically necessitate a separate children's assessment however, since meeting the support needs of the adult with parenting responsibilities is intended to prevent the child becoming a child 'in need'.

The identification that a child is regularly undertaking excessive or inappropriate care tasks in respect of a disabled parent should automatically trigger an assessment of the adult's personal support needs, including any assistance needed with parenting tasks. Assessment using the *Framework for the Assessment of Children in Need and their Families* should not take place as a matter of course, but only where it is deemed that certain needs of the child's are likely to remain unmet even when the parental support needs have been addressed.

Fair Access to Care Services: including parenting roles and responsibilities in Community Care needs assessment

The *Fair Access to Care Services* (FACS) policy guidance issued in 2002 by the Department of Health (2002a) specifies that a disabled adult's social and family roles should be taken into account when assessing the need for services but does not state that this should include parenting.

The omission of any explicit reference to parenting in the FACS Policy Guidance could mean that services to support disabled adults in their parenting role will remain a source of dispute within many social services departments. The danger is that adult services continue to maintain that children's services is the more relevant cost centre for parenting support whilst children's services continue to argue that unless and until a child is demonstrably in need, at risk or designated a 'young carer' the casework is not their responsibility.

More helpfully however, the FACS Practice Guidance (Questions and Answers p.5), clarifies that 'parenting roles and responsibilities' fall into those elements of the eligibility framework dealing with family and social roles and so it is clear that social services departments reviewing their eligibility criteria in the light of FACS are intended to ensure that parenting is covered by community care assessment.

The Human Rights Act 1998

Three of the more recent documents mentioned the Human Rights Act 1998. A number of provisions in this legislation are relevant to disabled parents including:

- Article 8: The right to respect for private and family life
- Article 12: The right to marry and to found a family
- Article 14: Upholding that the rights and freedoms set forth in the Act shall be secured without discrimination on any ground

The rights set out in the Human Rights Act 1998 are fully compatible with children's rights and the duty of the State (through local authorities) to safeguard and promote the welfare of children, as set out in the Children Act 1989.

references
grouped by:

- personal accounts
- publications based on primary research
- publications based on secondary research, including research and literature reviews
- other writing, including general, political and theoretical work and training materials
- writing on 'young carers'
- policy documents, Guidance and inspection reports

personal accounts

BILD (2000) *Good Times, Bad Times: Women with Learning Difficulties tell their Stories*. British Institute of Learning Disabilities

Bullivant, J. (2001) Lessons to be learnt, in *Disability, Pregnancy and Parenthood international* Journal 36(October)

Chowdry, S. (2002) *Deaf Parents: Gaps in Services* (BSL signed video). SCOPE (available from the Deaf Parenting project c/o *Disability, Pregnancy and Parenthood international*)

Disability, Pregnancy and Parenthood international journal from 1993 to present

DPPi (2001) Report of a day seminar on parents with learning difficulties held by the Department of Health, includes first hand accounts by mothers with learning difficulties, in *Disability, Pregnancy and Parenthood international* Journal 36(October)

Doe, T. (2002) Of sound mind; impossible expectations, in *Disability, Pregnancy and Parenthood international* Journal 40(October)

Finger, A. (1990) *Past Due: a Story of Disability, Pregnancy and Birth.* The Women's Press

Keith, L. (1994) (ed.) *Mustn't Grumble: Writing by Disabled Women.* The Women's Press

Mason, M. (1992) A nineteen parent family, in J. Morris (ed) *Alone Together: Voices of Single Parents.* The Women's Press

Morris, J. (1992) Feeling special, in J. Morris (ed.) *Alone Together: Voices of Single Parents.* The Women's Press

O'Toole, C.J. and D'aoust, V. (2000) Fit for motherhood: towards a recognition of multiplicity in disabled lesbian mothers, in *Disability Studies Quarterly* 20(2)

Preston, P. (1995) *Mother Father Deaf: Living between Sound and Silence.* Harvard University Press

Shackle, M. (1993) *I Thought I was the Only One: Report of a Conference 'Disabled people, pregnancy and early parenthood'.* Maternity Alliance

Sherer-Jacobson, D. (1999) *The Question of David*. Creative Arts Books

Sikand, M. (2002) Roller coaster ride: questions but no answers, in *Disability, Pregnancy and Parenthood international* Journal 40(October)

Wates, M. and Jade, R. (1999) *Bigger than the Sky: Disabled Women on Parenting*. The Women's Press

publications based on primary research

Aldgate, J. and Bradley, M. (1999) *Supporting Families through Short-term Fostering*. The Stationery Office

Alexander, C., Hwang, K. and Sipski, M. (2002) Mothers with spinal cord injuries: impact on marital, family and children's adjustment, in *Archives of Physical Medicine and Rehabilitation* 83

Bebbington, A. and Miles, J. (1989) The background of children who enter care, in *British Journal of Social Work* 19(5)

Booth, T. and Booth, W. (1993a) Parenting with learning difficulties: lessons for practitioners, in *British Journal of Social Work* 23

Booth, W. and Booth, T. (1993b) Learning the hard way: practice issues in supporting parents with learning difficulties, in *Social Work and Social Sciences Review* 4(2)

Booth, T. and Booth, W. (1994a) Parental adequacy, parenting failure and parents with learning difficulties, in *Health and Social Care in the Community* 2(3)

Booth, T. and Booth, W. (1994b) *Parenting under Pressure: Mothers and Fathers with Learning Disabilities*. Open University Press

Booth, T. and Booth, W. (1998a) *Growing up with Parents who have Learning Difficulties*. Routledge

Booth, W. and Booth, T. (1998b) *Advocacy for Parents with Learning Difficulties: Developing Advocacy Support*. Pavilion Publishing (with the Joseph Rowntree Foundation)

Brandon, M., Thoburn, J., Lewis, A. and Way, A. (1999) *Safeguarding Children with the Children Act 1989*. The Stationery Office

Brandt, P. and Weinert, C. (1998) Children's mental health in families experiencing multiple sclerosis, in *Journal of Family Nursing*, 4(1)

Falkov, A. (1996) *Study of Working Together Part 8 Reports. Fatal Child Abuse and Parental Psychiatric Disorder: An Analysis of 100 Area Child Protection Committee Case Reviews Conducted under the Terms of Part 8 of Working Together under the Children Act 1989*. Department of Health

Feldman, M. and Walton-Allen, N. (1997) Effects of maternal mental retardation and poverty on intellectual, academic and behavioural status of school-age children, in *American Journal on Mental Retardation* 101

Feldman, M., Varghese, J., Ramsay, J. and Rajska, D. (2002) Relationships between social support, stress and mother-child interactions in mothers with intellectual disabilities, in *Journal of Applied Research in Intellectual Disabilities* 15

Gibbons, J., Conroy, S. and Bell, C. (1995) *Operating the Child Protection System*. HMSO

Gordon, D., Adelman, L., Ashworth, K., Bradshaw, J., Levitas, R., Middleton, S., Pantazis, C., Patsios, D., Payne, S., Townsend, P. and Williams, J. (2000) *Poverty and Social Exclusion in Britain*. Joseph Rowntree Foundation

Hawes, V. and Cottrell, D. (1999) Disruption of children's lives by maternal psychiatric admission, in *Psychiatric Bulletin* 23

Henricson, C. (ed.) (2002) *Reaching Parents: Producing and Delivering Parent Information Resources*. National Family and Parenting Institute

Henricson, C., Katz, I., Mesie, J., Sandison, M. and Tunstill, J. (2001) *National Mapping of Family Services in England and Wales: A Consultation Document*. National Family and Parenting Institute

Hirsch, B., Moos, R. and Reischl, T. (1985) Psychosocial adjustment of adolescent children of a depressed, arthritic, or normal parent, in *Journal of Abnormal Psychology* 94(2)

Isaac, B., Minty, E. and Morrison, R. (1986) Children in care: the association with mental disorder in parents, in *British Journal of Social Work* 16

James, G. (1994) *Department of Health Discussion Report for ACPC Conference: Study of Working Together Part 8 Reports*. Department of Health

Jamison, R. and Walker, L. (1992) Illness behaviour in children of chronic pain patients, in *International Journal of Psychiatry in Medicine* 22(4)

Kearney, P., Levin, E. and Rosen, G. (2000) *Working With Families: Alcohol, Drugs and Mental Health Problems. A Research and Development Report*. NISW (re-publishing in 2003 as SCIE Report no 2)

LeClere, F. and Kowalewski, B. (1994) Disability in the family: the effects on children's well-being, in *Journal of Marriage and the Family* 56(May)

McConnell, D., Llewellyn, G. and Ferronato, L. (2002) Disability and decision-making in Australian care proceedings, in *International Journal of Law, Policy and the Family* 16

Olsen, R. and Clarke, H. (2003) *Parenting and Disability: Disabled Parents' Experiences of Raising Children*. The Policy Press

Olsen, R. and Tyers, H. (2003, forthcoming) *Sharing Good Practice in Supporting Disabled Parents*. National Family and Parenting Institute

Partridge, A. (2001) *Supporting Families Research Project: Parents with Mental Health or Substance Misuse Problems and their Dependent Children.* Oxfordshire Social Services Department

Quinton, D. and Rutter, M. (1984) Parents with children in care: current circumstances and parenting, in *Journal of Child Psychology and Psychiatry* 25

Radke-Yarrow, M. (1991) *Attachment Patterns in Children of Depressed Mothers.* Routledge

Robinson, S., Hickson, F. and Strike, R. (2001) *More Than Getting Through The Gate: The Involvement of Parents who have a Disability in their Children's School Education in NSW.* Disability Council of NSW

Roker, D. and Coleman, J. (1998) 'Parenting teenagers' programmes: a UK perspective, in *Children and Society* 12

Sheppard, M. (1997) Double jeopardy: the link between child abuse and maternal depression in child and family social work, in *Child and Family Social Work* 2

Sheppard, M. (2002) Depressed mothers' experience of partnership in child and family care, in *British Journal of Social Work* 32

Stanley, N. and Penhale, B. (1999) The mental health problems of mothers experiencing the child protection system: identifying needs and appropriate responses, in *Child Abuse Review* 8

Thoburn, J., Lewis, A. and Shemmings, D. (1995) *Paternalism or Partnership? Family Involvement in the Child Protection Process.* HMSO

Toms-Barker, L. and Maralani V. (1977) *Challenges and Strategies of Disabled Parents: Findings from a National Survey of Parents with Disabilities.* Through the Looking Glass

Tracey, B.L. (2002) *Silent Partners? The problems for Deaf parents in accessing appropriate information and support from Health, Education and Social Services for themselves and their (predominantly) hearing children.* Submitted as BSc Third Year dissertation, University of Bristol School for Policy Studies

Tunstill, J. and Aldgate, J. (2000) *Services for Children in Need: From Policy to Practice.* The Stationery Office

Wang, A. and Goldschmidt, V. (1994) Interviews of psychiatric inpatients about their family situation and young children, in *Acta Psychiatrica Scandinavica* 90

Wates, M. (1997) *Disabled Parents: Dispelling the Myths.* National Childbirth Trust/Radcliffe Medical Press

Wates, M. (2002) *Supporting Disabled Adults in their Parenting Role.* Joseph Rowntree Foundation

Wates, M. (2003) *It shouldn't be down to luck*. A report on a consultation with disabled parents for Disabled Parents Network. Full text, summary report and brief summary in plain English available from www.DisabledParentsNetwork.org.uk

Weiner, M. (2002) *Understanding Deaf Parents with Hearing Children*. Paper presented at the 2nd International conference on disabled parenting, California 2002 and reviewed in *Disability, Pregnancy and Parenthood international* Journal 40 (October)

White, C. and Barrowclough, C. (1998) Depressed and non-depressed mothers with problematic preschoolers: attributions for child behaviours, in *British Journal of Clinical Psychology* 37(4)

publications based on secondary research, including research and literature reviews

Aldgate, J. and Statham, J. (2001) *The Children Act Now: Messages from Research*. The Stationery Office

Andron, L. and Tymchuk, A. (1987) Parents who are mentally retarded, in Craft, A. (ed.) *Mental Handicap and Sexuality*. Costello

Belsky, J., Robins, E. and Gamble, W. (1984) The determinants of parental competence: towards a contextual theory, in Lewis, M. (ed.) *Beyond the Dyad*. Plenum Press

Bleuler, M. (1978) *The Schizophrenic Disorders: Long-Term Patient and Family Studies*. Yale University Press

Cleaver, H., Unell, I. and Aldgate, J. (1999) *Children's Needs - Parenting Capacity: The Impact of Parental Mental Illness, Problem Alcohol and Drug Use, and Domestic Violence on Children's Development*. The Stationery Office

Dartington Social Research Unit (1995) *Child Protection: Messages from Research*. HMSO

Dowdney, L. and Skuse, D. (1993) Parenting provided by adults with mental retardation, in *Journal of Child Psychology and Psychiatry* 34

McGaw, S. (2000) *What Works for Parents with Learning Disabilities?* Barnardo's

Mizen, P., Bolton, A. and Pole, C. (1999) School age workers: the paid employment of children in Britain, in *Work, Employment and Society* 13(3)

Newman, T. (2002) *Promoting Resilience: A Review of Effective Strategies for Child Care Services*. Centre for Evidence Based Social Services

Parton, N. (1997) Child protection and family support: current debates and future prospects, in Parton, N. (ed.) *Child Protection and Family Support*. Routledge

Roy, R. (1990) Consequences of parental illness on children: a review, in *Social Work and Social Sciences Review* 2(2)

Steck, B. (2000) The Psychosocial impact of multiple sclerosis on families and children, in *International Multiple Sclerosis Journal* 7(2)

Vondra, J. and Belsky, J. (1993) Developmental origins of parenting: personality and relationship factors, in T. Luster and L. Okagaki (eds) *Parenting: An Ecological Perspective.* Lawrence Erlbaum Associates

Webster-Stratton, C. (1999) Researching the impact of parent training programmes on child conduct problems, in E. Lloyd (ed.) (1999) *Parenting Matters: What Works in Parenting Education?* Barnardo's

other writing, including general, political and theoretical work and training materials

Bailey, K. (2003, forthcoming) Learning More from the Social Model: linking experience, participation and knowledge production, in Barnes, C. and Mercer, G. (eds) (2003, forthcoming) *The Social Model of Disability: Theory and research.* The Disability Press

Barnes, C. (2003) What a Difference a Decade Makes: reflections on doing 'emancipatory' disability research, in *Disability and Society* 18

Barnes, C. and Mercer, G. (eds) (2003, forthcoming) *The Social Model of Disability: Theory and research.* The Disability Press

Bignall, T., Box, L. and Otoo, S. (2001) *Family support for parents and families with additional needs.* REU Discussion Paper 7

BILD (2002) *Pregnancy and Childbirth,* booklet forming part of BILD's *Your Good Health Series*

Block, P. (2002) editorial feature on parenting including work by Block, P., Fitzmaurice, S., Kent, D., O'Toole, C., Doe, T., Kirschbaum, M., Olkins, R. and Ehlers-Flint, M. *Sexuality and Disability.* Spring

Bronfenbrenner, U. (1979) *The Ecology of Human Development: Experiments by Nature and Design.* Harvard University Press

Campion, M. (1995) *Who's Fit to be a Parent?* Routledge

Corker, M. (1999) New disability discourse, the principle of optimisation and social change, in Corker, M. and French, S. (eds) *Disability Discourses.* Open University Press

Department of Health (1998) *Crossing Bridges: Training Resources for Working with Mentally Ill Parents and their Children.* Pavilion

Ferguson, P., Gartner, A. and Lipsky, D. (2000) The experience of disability in families: a synthesis of research and parent narratives in Parens, E. and Asch, A. (eds) *Prenatal Testing and Disability Rights.* Georgetown University Press

Finkelstein, V. (1992) *Researching Disability: Setting the Agenda for Change.* A paper at the 'Setting Future Agendas' Conference, Centre for Disability Studies Archive www.leeds.ac.uk/disability-studies/archiveuk/finkelstein/futures.pdf

Guldberg, H. (2000) Child protection and the precautionary principle, in Morris, J. (ed.) *Rethinking Risk and the Precautionary Principle.* Butterworth/Heinneman

Henricson, C. (2003) *Government and Parenting: Is there a Case for a Policy Review and a Parents' Code?* Joseph Rowntree Foundation

Iqbal, S. (2004 forthcoming) *Pregnancy and Birth: a guide for deaf women.* Royal National Institute for the Deaf (RNID)

Jones. R., Keep, J. and Wates, M. (2003) The social context of impairment' in *Inform* ADSS (April)

McGaw, S. (1995) '*I want to be a good parent...*' BILD (a series of workbooks designed for use with learning disabled parents or prospective parents)

Mercer, G. (2002) Emancipatory disability research, in Barnes, C., Oliver, M. and Barton, L. (eds) *Disability Studies Today.* Policy Press

Mercer, G. (2003 forthcoming) To Research or Not to Research? Is that the Question for Disability Studies?, in Barnes, C. and Mercer, G. *The Social Model of Disability: Theory and research.* The Disability Press

Morris, J. (2003, forthcoming) *The Right Support: Report of the Task Force on Disabled Adults and Parenting.* Joseph Rowntree Foundation

Newman, T. and Wates, M. (eds) (2003 forthcoming) *Disabled Parents and their Children: building a better future* (provisional title). Barnardo's

Olkin, R. (1999) *What Psychotherapists Should Know about Disability.* The Guildford Press

Oliver, M. (1992) Changing the social relations of research production? in *Disability, Handicap and Society* 7(2)

Parens, E. and Asch, A. (eds) (2000) *Prenatal Testing and Disability Rights.* Georgetown University Press

Pawson, R., Barnes, C., Boaz, A., Grayson, L., Long, A. (2003), *Types and Quality of Social Care Knowledge.* ESRC UK Centre for Evidence Based Policy and Practice: Working Paper 17

Ricability (2000) *Equipped? Report of a Survey about Childcare Equipment and Disabled Parents.* Ricability

Sample, P. (1996) Beginnings: participatory action research and adults with developmental disabilities, in *Ability and Society* 11(3)

Sayce, L. (1999) Parenting as a civil right: Supporting service users who choose to have children, in Weir, A. and Douglas, A. (eds) *Child Protection and Adult Mental Health: Conflict of Interest?* Butterworth-Heinemann

Smith, C. (1997) *Developing Parenting Programmes.* National Children's Bureau

Stalker, K. (1998) Some ethical and methodological issues in research with people with learning difficulties, in *Disability and Society* 13(1)

Tanner, D. (2000) Crossing bridges over troubled waters?: working with children of parents experiencing mental distress, in *Social Work Education* 19(3)

Vensand, K., Rogers, J., Tuleja, C. and DeMoss, A. (2000) *Adaptive Baby Care Equipment: Guidelines, Prototypes & Resources*. Through the Looking Glass

writing on 'young carers'

Aldridge, J. and Becker, S. (1993) *Children who Care; Inside the World of Young Carers*. Loughborough University

Aldridge, J. and Becker, S. (1994) *My Child, My Carer; the Parents' Perspective*. Loughborough University

Aldridge, J. and Becker, S. (2003) *Children Caring for Parents with Mental Illness: Perspectives of Young Carers, Parents and Professionals*. Bristol

Aldridge, J and Wates, M. (2003, forthcoming) Disabled parents and young carers: moving the debate on, in Newman, T. and Wates, M. (eds) *Disabled Parents and their Children: Building a better future* (provisional title). Barnardo's

Becker, S., Aldridge, J. and Dearden, C. (1998) *Young Carers and their Families*. Blackwell Science

Bilsborrow, S. (1992) *You Grow Up Fast As Well...Young Carers on Merseyside (3rd draft)*. Barnardo's

Crabtree, H. and Warner, L. (1999) *Too Much to Take On: A Report on Young Carers and Bullying*. The Princess Royal Trust for Carers

Madge, N., Burton, S., Howell, S. and Hearn, B. (2000) *9-13: The Forgotten Years?* National Children's Bureau

Dearden, C. and Becker, S. (1995) *Young Carers: The Facts*. Reed Business Publishing

Dearden, C. and Becker, S. (2000) *Growing up Caring: Vulnerability and Transition to Adulthood; Young Carers' Experiences*. Youth Work Press with the Joseph Rowntree Foundation

Fox, N. (1995) Professional models of school absence associated with home responsibilities, in *British Journal of Sociology of Education* 16(2)

Fox, N. (1998) The contribution of children to informal care: a Delphi study, in *Health and Social Care in the Community* 6(3)

Frank, J. (1995) *Couldn't Care More: A Study of Young Carers and their Needs*. The Children's Society

Gradwell, L. (1992) The parent's tale, in *Coalition*, September

Jones, A., Jeyasingham, D. and Rajasooriya, S. (2002) *Invisible Families: The Strengths and Needs of Black Families in which Young People have Caring Responsibilities*. The Policy Press

Keith, L. and Morris, J. (1996) Easy targets: a disability rights perspective on the 'children as carers' debate, in *Critical Social Policy* 45

Meredith, H. (1992) *The Young Carers Project: A Report on Achievements 1990-1992.* Carers National Association

Olsen, R. (1996) Young carers: challenging the facts and politics of research into children and caring, in *Disability and Society* 11(1)

Olsen, R. (2000) Families under the microscope: parallels between the 'young carers' debate of the 1990s and the removal of children from the industrial labour force in the 19th century, in *Children and Society* 14

Olsen, R. and Parker, G. (1997) 'A response to Aldridge and Becker - 'Disability rights and the denial of young carers: the dangers of zero-sum arguments'', in *Critical Social Policy* 17(1)

Shah, R. and Hatton, C. (1999) *Caring Alone: Young Carers in South Asian Communities.* Barnardo's

Stables, J. and Smith, F. (1999) Caught in the 'Cinderella Trap': Narratives of Disabled Parents and Young Carers', in Butler, R. and Parr, (eds) *Mind and Body Spaces: Geographies of Illness, Impairment and Disability.* Routledge

Wates, M. (2001) *Disabled parents and the 'young carers' issue.* Paper given at an NCH conference for young carers project workers, York 2001 www.DisabledParentsNetwork.org.uk

government documents, Guidance and inspection reports
Department of Health (1995) *Young Carers* Chief Inspector's letter CI (95) 12

Department of Health (2001) *Valuing People: A New Strategy for Learning Disability in the 21st Century (CM 5086).* The Stationery Office

Department of Health (2002a) *Fair Access to Care Services.* Practice Guidance. Department of Health

Department of Health (2002b) *Fair Access to Care Services.* Guidance on Eligibility Criteria for Adult Social Care. LAC(2002)13. Department of Health

Department of Health, Department for Education and Employment and Home Office (2000) *Framework for the Assessment of Children in Need and their Families.* The Stationery Office

Department of Health (2000) *Assessing Children in Need and their Families: Practice guidance,* The Stationery Office

Department of Work and Pensions (2001) *Economic activity status of disabled people: by gender,* Spring 2001: Social Trends 32 http://www.statistics.gov.uk/STATBASE/ssdataset.asp?vlnk=5094

Goodinge, S. (2000) *A Jigsaw of Services: Inspection of Services to Support Disabled Adults in their Parenting Role.* Department of Health

references, listed alphabetically, by author

Aldgate, J. and Bradley, M. (1999) *Supporting Families through Short-term Fostering.* The Stationery Office

Aldgate, J. and Statham, J. (2001) *The Children Act Now: Messages from Research.* The Stationery Office

Aldridge, J. and Becker, S. (1993) *Children who Care; Inside the World of Young Carers.* Loughborough University

Aldridge, J. and Becker, S. (1994) *My Child, My Carer; the Parents' Perspective.* Loughborough University

Aldridge, J. and Becker, S. (2003) *Children Caring for Parents with Mental Illness: Perspectives of Young Carers, Parents and Professionals.* Bristol

Aldridge, J and Wates, M. (2003, forthcoming) Disabled parents and young carers: moving the debate on, in Newman, T. and Wates, M. (eds) *Disabled Parents and their Children: Building a better future.* (provisional title). Barnardo's

Alexander, C., Hwang, K. and Sipski, M. (2002) Mothers with spinal cord injuries: impact on marital, family and children's adjustment, in *Archives of Physical Medicine and Rehabilitation 83*

Andron, L. and Tymchuk, A. (1987) Parents who are mentally retarded, in Craft, A. (ed.) *Mental Handicap and Sexuality.* Costello

Bailey, K. (2003, forthcoming) Learning More from the Social Model: linking experience, participation and knowledge production, in Barnes, C. and Mercer, G. (eds) (2003, forthcoming) *The Social Model of Disability: Theory and research.* The Disability Press

Barnes, C. (2003) What a difference a Decade Makes: reflections on doing 'emancipatory' disability research, in *Disability and Society 18*

Barnes, C. and Mercer, G. (eds) (2003, forthcoming) *The Social Model of Disability: Theory and research.* The Disability Press

Bebbington, A. and Miles, J. (1989) The background of children who enter care, in *British Journal of Social Work 19(5)*

Becker, S., Aldridge, J. and Dearden, C. (1998) *Young Carers and their Families.* Blackwell Science

Belsky, J., Robins, E. and Gamble, W. (1984) The determinants of parental competence: towards a contextual theory, in Lewis, M. (ed.) *Beyond the Dyad.* Plenum Press

Bignall, T., Box, L. and Otoo, S. (2001) *Family support for parents and families with addional needs.* REU Discussion Paper 7

BILD (2000) *Good Times, Bad Times: Women with Learning Difficulties tell their Stories.* British Institute of Learning Disabilities

BILD (2002) *Pregnancy and Childbirth,* booklet forming part of BILD's *Your Good Health* series

Bilsborrow, S. (1992) *You Grow Up Fast As Well...Young Carers on Merseyside (3rd draft)*. Barnardo's

Bleuler, M. (1978) *The Schizophrenic Disorders: Long-Term Patient and Family Studies*. Yale University Press

Block, P. (2002) editor feature on parenting including work by Block, P., Fitzmaurice, S., Kent, D., O'Toole, C., Doe, T., Kirschbaum, M., Olkins, R. and Ehlers-Flint, M. *Sexuality and Disability*. Spring

Booth, T. and Booth, W. (1993a) Parenting with learning difficulties: lessons for practitioners, in *British Journal of Social Work* 23

Booth, T. and Booth, W. (1994a) Parental adequacy, parenting failure and parents with learning difficulties, in *Health and Social Care in the Community* 2(3)

Booth, T. and Booth, W. (1994b) *Parenting under Pressure: Mothers and Fathers with Learning Disabilities*. Open University Press

Booth, T. and Booth, W. (1998a) *Growing up with Parents who have Learning Difficulties*. Routledge

Booth, W. and Booth, T. (1993b) Learning the hard way: practice issues in supporting parents with learning difficulties, in *Social Work and Social Sciences Review* 4(2)

Booth, W. and Booth, T. (1998b) *Advocacy for Parents with Learning Difficulties: Developing Advocacy Support*. Pavilion Publishing (with the Joseph Rowntree Foundation)

Brandon, M., Thoburn, J., Lewis, A. and Way, A. (1999) *Safeguarding Children with the Children Act 1989*. The Stationery Office

Brandt, P. and Weinert, C. (1998) Children's mental health in families experiencing multiple sclerosis, in *Journal of Family Nursing*, 4(1)

Bronfenbrenner, U. (1979) *The Ecology of Human Development: Experiments by Nature and Design*. Harvard University Press

Bullivant, J. (2001) Lessons to be learnt, in *Disability, Pregnancy and Parenthood international* Journal 36(October)

Campion, M. (1995) *Who's Fit to be a Parent?* Routledge

Chowdry, S. (2002) *Deaf Parents: Gaps in Services* (BSL signed video). SCOPE (available from the Deaf Parenting project c/o Disability, Pregnancy and Parenthood international)

Cleaver, H., Unell, I. and Aldgate, J. (1999) *Children's Needs - Parenting Capacity: The Impact of Parental Mental Illness, Problem Alcohol and Drug Use, and Domestic Violence on Children's Development*. The Stationery Office

Corker, M. (1999) New disability discourse, the principle of optimisation and social change, in Corker, M. and French, S. (eds) *Disability Discourses*. Open University Press

Crabtree, H. and Warner, L. (1999) *Too Much to Take On: A Report on Young Carers and Bullying*. The Princess Royal Trust for Carers

Dartington Social Research Unit (1995) *Child Protection: Messages from Research*. HMSO

Dearden, C. and Becker, S. (1995) *Young Carers: The Facts*. Reed Business Publishing

Dearden, C. and Becker, S. (2000) *Growing up Caring: Vulnerability and Transition to Adulthood; Young Carers' Experiences*. Youth Work Press with the Joseph Rowntree Foundation

Department of Health (1995) *Young Carers* Chief Inspector's letter CI (95) 12

Department of Health (1998) *Crossing Bridges: Training Resources for Working with Mentally Ill Parents and their Children*. Pavilion

Department of Health (2001) *Valuing People: A New Strategy for Learning Disability in the 21st Century (CM 5086)*. The Stationery Office

Department of Health (2002a) *Fair Access to Care Services*. Practice Guidance. Department of Health

Department of Health (2002b) *Fair Access to Care Services*. Guidance on Eligibility Criteria for Adult Social Care. LAC(2002)13. Department of Health

Department of Health, Department for Education and Employment and Home Office (2000) *Framework for the Assessment of Children in Need and their Families*. The Stationery Office

Department of Work and Pensions (2001) *Economic activity status of disabled people: by gender*, Spring 2001: Social Trends 32 http://www.statistics.gov.uk/STATBASE/ssdataset.asp?vlnk=5094

Disability, Pregnancy and Parenthood international journal from 1993 to present

Doe, T. (2002) Of sound mind; impossible expectations, in *Disability, Pregnancy and Parenthood* international Journal 40(October)

Dowdney, L. and Skuse, D. (1993) Parenting provided by adults with mental retardation, in *Journal of Child Psychology and Psychiatry* 34

DPPi (2001) Report of a day seminar on parents with learning difficulties held by the Department of Health, includes first hand accounts by mothers with learning difficulties, in *Disability, Pregnancy and Parenthood* international Journal 36 (October)

Falkov, A. (1996) *Study of Working Together Part 8 Reports. Fatal Child Abuse and Parental Psychiatric Disorder: An Analysis of 100 Area Child Protection Committee Case Reviews Conducted under the Terms of Part 8 of Working Together under the Children Act 1989*. Department of Health

Feldman, M. and Walton-Allen, N. (1997) Effects of maternal mental retardation and poverty on intellectual, academic and behavioural status of school-age children, in *American Journal on Mental Retardation* 101

Feldman, M., Varghese, J., Ramsay, J. and Rajska, D. (2002) Relationships between social support, stress and mother-child interactions in mothers with intellectual disabilities, in *Journal of Applied Research in Intellectual Disabilities* 15

Ferguson, P., Gartner, A. and Lipsky, D. (2000) The experience of disability in families: a synthesis of research and parent narratives in Parens, E. and Asch, A. (eds) *Prenatal Testing and Disability Rights.* Georgetown University Press

Finger, A. (1990) *Past Due: a Story of Disability, Pregnancy and Birth.* The Women's Press

Finkelstein, V. (1992) *Researching Disability: Setting the Agenda for Change.* A paper at the 'Setting Future Agendas' Conference, Centre for Disability Studies Archive www.leeds.ac.uk/disability-studies/archiveuk/finkelstein/futures.pdf

Fox, N. (1995) Professional models of school absence associated with home responsibilities, in *British Journal of Sociology of Education* 16(2)

Fox, N. (1998) The contribution of children to informal care: a Delphi study, in *Health and Social Care in the Community* 6(3)

Frank, J. (1995) *Couldn't Care More: A Study of Young Carers and their Needs.* The Children's Society

Gibbons, J., Conroy, S. and Bell, C. (1995) *Operating the Child Protection System. HMSO*

Goodinge, S. (2000) *A Jigsaw of Services: Inspection of Services to Support Disabled Adults in their Parenting Role.* Department of Health

Gordon, D., Adelman, L., Ashworth, K., Bradshaw, J., Levitas, R., Middleton, S., Pantazis, C., Patsios, D., Payne, S., Townsend, P. and Williams, J. (2000) *Poverty and Social Exclusion in Britain.* Joseph Rowntree Foundation

Gradwell, L. (1992) The parent's tale, in *Coalition, September*

Guldberg, H. (2000) Child protection and the precautionary principle, in Morris, J. (ed.) *Rethinking Risk and the Precautionary Principle.* Butterworth/Heinneman

Hawes, V. and Cottrell, D. (1999) Disruption of children's lives by maternal psychiatric admission, in *Psychiatric Bulletin* 23

Henricson, C. (ed.) (2002) *Reaching Parents: Producing and Delivering Parent Information Resources.* National Family and Parenting Institute

Henricson, C. (2003) *Government and Parenting: Is there a Case for a Policy Review and a Parents' Code?* Joseph Rowntree Foundation

Henricson, C., Katz, I., Mesie, J., Sandison, M. and Tunstill, J. (2001) *National Mapping of Family Services in England and Wales: A Consultation Document*. National Family and Parenting Institute

Hirsch, B., Moos, R. and Reischl, T. (1985) Psychosocial adjustment of adolescent children of a depressed, arthritic, or normal parent, in *Journal of Abnormal Psychology* 94(2)

Iqbal, S. (2004 forthcoming) *Pregnancy and Birth: a guide for deaf women*. Royal National Institute for the Deaf (RNID)

Isaac, B., Minty, E. and Morrison, R. (1986) Children in care: the association with mental disorder in parents, in *British Journal of Social Work* 16

James, G. (1994) *Department of Health Discussion Report for ACPC Conference: Study of Working Together Part 8 Reports*. Department of Health

Jamison, R. and Walker, L. (1992) Illness behaviour in children of chronic pain patients, in *International Journal of Psychiatry in Medicine* 22(4)

Jones, A., Jeyasingham, D. and Rajasooriya, S. (2002) *Invisible Families: The Strengths and Needs of Black Families in which Young People have Caring Responsibilities*. The Policy Press

Jones. R., Keep, J. and Wates, M. (2003) The social context of impairment' in *Inform* ADSS (April)

Kearney, P., Levin, E. and Rosen, G. (2000) *Working With Families: Alcohol, Drugs and Mental Health Problems. A Research and Development Report*. NISW (re-publishing in 2003 as SCIE Report no 2)

Keith, L. (1994) (ed.) *Mustn't Grumble: Writing by Disabled Women*. The Women's Press

Keith, L. and Morris, J. (1996) Easy targets: a disability rights perspective on the 'children as carers' debate, in *Critical Social Policy* 45

LeClere, F. and Kowalewski, B. (1994) Disability in the family: the effects on children's well-being, in *Journal of Marriage and the Family* 56(May)

McConnell, D., Llewellyn, G. and Ferronato, L. (2002) Disability and decision-making in Australian care proceedings, in *International Journal of Law, Policy and the Family* 16

McGaw, S. (1995) *'I want to be a good parent...'* BILD (a series of workbooks designed for use with learning disabled parents or prospective parents)

McGaw, S. (2000) *What Works for Parents with Learning Disabilities?* Barnardo's

Madge, N., Burton, S., Howell, S. and Hearn, B. (2000) *9-13: The Forgotten Years?* National Children's Bureau

Mason, M. (1992) A nineteen parent family, in J. Morris (ed.) *Alone Together: Voices of Single Parents.* The Women's Press

Mercer, G. (2002) Emancipatory disability research, in Barnes, C., Oliver, M. and Barton, L. (eds) *Disability Studies Today.* Policy Press

Mercer, G. (2003 forthcoming) To Research or Not to Research? Is that the Question for Disability Studies?, in Barnes, C. and Mercer, G. *The Social Model of Disability: Theory and research.* The Disability Press

Meredith, H. (1992) *The Young Carers Project: A Report on Achievements 1990-1992.* Carers National Association

Mizen, P., Bolton, A. and Pole, C. (1999) School age workers: the paid employment of children in Britain, in *Work, Employment and Society* 13(3)

Morris, J. (1992) Feeling special, in J. Morris (ed.) *Alone Together: Voices of Single Parents.* The Women's Press

Morris, J. (2003, forthcoming) *The Right Support: Report of the Task Force on Disabled Adults and Parenting.* Joseph Rowntree Foundation

Newman, T. (2002) *Promoting Resilience: A Review of Effective Strategies for Child Care Services.* Centre for Evidence Based Social Services

Newman, T. and Wates, M. (eds) (2003 forthcoming) *Disabled Parents and their Children: building a better future* (provisional title). Barnardo's

O'Toole, C.J. and D'aoust, V. (2000) Fit for motherhood: towards a recognition of multiplicity in disabled lesbian mothers, in *Disability Studies Quarterly* 20(2)

Oliver, M. (1992) Changing the social relations of research production? in *Disability, Handicap and Society* 7(2)

Olkin, R. (1999) *What Psychotherapists Should Know about Disability.* The Guildford Press

Olsen, R. (1996) Young carers: challenging the facts and politics of research into children and caring, in *Disability and Society* 11(1)

Olsen, R. (2000) Families under the microscope: parallels between the 'young carers' debate of the 1990s and the removal of children from the industrial labour force in the 19th century, in *Children and Society* 14

Olsen, R. and Clarke, H. (2003) *Parenting and Disability: Disabled Parents' Experiences of Raising Children.* The Policy Press

Olsen, R. and Parker, G. (1997) 'A response to Aldridge and Becker - 'Disability rights and the denial of young carers: the dangers of zero-sum arguments'', in *Critical Social Policy* 17(1)

Olsen, R. and Tyers, H. (2003, forthcoming) *Sharing Good Practice in Supporting Disabled Parents.* National Family and Parenting Institute

Parens, E. and Asch, A. (eds) (2000) *Prenatal Testing and Disability Rights.* Georgetown University Press

Parton, N. (1997) Child protection and family support: current debates and future prospects in Parton, N. (ed.) *Child Protection and Family Support*. Routledge

Partridge, A. (2001) *Supporting Families Research Project: Parents with Mental Health or Substance Misuse Problems and their Dependent Children.* Oxfordshire Social Services Department

Pawson, R., Barnes, C., Boaz, A., Grayson, L., Long, A. (2003), *Types and Quality of Social Care Knowledge.* ESRC UK Centre for Evidence Based Policy and Practice: Working Paper 17

Preston, P. (1995) *Mother Father Deaf: Living between Sound and Silence.* Harvard University Press

Quinton, D. and Rutter, M. (1984) Parents with children in care: current circumstances and parenting, in *Journal of Child Psychology and Psychiatry* 25

Radke-Yarrow, M. (1991) *Attachment Patterns in Children of Depressed Mothers.* Routledge

Ricability (2000) *Equipped? Report of a Survey about Childcare Equipment and Disabled Parents.* Ricability

Robinson, S., Hickson, F., and Strike, R. (2001) *More Than Getting Through The Gate: The Involvement of Parents who have a Disability in their Children's School Education in NSW.* Disability Council of NSW

Roker, D. and Coleman, J. (1998) 'Parenting teenagers' programmes: a UK perspective, in *Children and Society* 12

Roy, R. (1990) Consequences of parental illness on children: a review, in *Social Work and Social Sciences Review* 2(2)

Sample, P. (1996) Beginnings: participatory action research and adults with developmental disabilities, in *Ability and Society* 11(3)

Sayce, L. (1999) Parenting as a civil right: Supporting service users who choose to have children, in Weir, A. and Douglas, A. (eds) *Child Protection and Adult Mental Health: Conflict of Interest?* Butterworth-Heinemann

Shackle, M. (1993) *I Thought I was the Only One: Report of a Conference 'Disabled people, pregnancy and early parenthood'.* Maternity Alliance

Shah, R. and Hatton, C. (1999) *Caring Alone: Young Carers in South Asian Communities.* Barnardo's

Sheppard, M. (1997) Double jeopardy: the link between child abuse and maternal depression in child and family social work, in *Child and Family Social Work* 2

Sheppard, M. (2002) Depressed mothers' experience of partnership in child and family care, in *British Journal of Social Work* 32

Sherer-Jacobson, D. (1999) *The Question of David*. Creative Arts Books

Sikand, M. (2002) Roller coaster ride: questions but no answers, in *Disability, Pregnancy and Parenthood international* Journal 40 (October)

Smith, C. (1997) *Developing Parenting Programmes*. National Children's Bureau

Stables, J. and Smith, F. (1999) Caught in the 'Cinderella Trap': Narratives of Disabled Parents and Young Carers', in Butler, R. and Parr, (eds) *Mind and Body Spaces: Geographies of Illness, Impairment and Disability*. Routledge

Stalker, K. (1998) Some ethical and methodological issues in research with people with learning difficulties, in *Disability and Society* 13(1)

Stanley, N. and Penhale, B. (1999) The mental health problems of mothers experiencing the child protection system: identifying needs and appropriate responses, in *Child Abuse Review* 8

Steck, B. (2000) The Psychosocial impact of multiple sclerosis on families and children, in *International Multiple Sclerosis Journal* 7(2)

Tanner, D. (2000) Crossing bridges over troubled waters?: working with children of parents experiencing mental distress, in *Social Work Education* 19(3)

Thoburn, J., Lewis, A. and Shemmings, D. (1995) *Paternalism or Partnership? Family Involvement in the Child Protection Process*. HMSO

Toms-Barker, L. and Maralani V. (1977) *Challenges and Strategies of Disabled Parents: Findings from a National Survey of Parents with Disabilities*. Through the Looking Glass

Tracey, B.L. (2002) *Silent Partners? The problems for Deaf parents in accessing appropriate information and support from Health, Education and Social Services for themselves and their (predominantly) hearing children*. Submitted as BSc Third Year dissertation, University of Bristol School for Policy Studies

Tunstill, J. and Aldgate, J. (2000) *Services for Children in Need: From Policy to Practice*. The Stationery Office

Vensand, K., Rogers, J., Tuleja, C. and DeMoss, A. (2000) *Adaptive Baby Care Equipment: Guidelines, Prototypes & Resources*. Through the Looking Glass

Vondra, J. and Belsky, J. (1993) Developmental origins of parenting: personality and relationship factors, in T. Luster and L. Okagaki (eds) *Parenting: An Ecological Perspective*. Lawrence Erlbaum Associates

Wang, A. and Goldschmidt, V. (1994) Interviews of psychiatric inpatients about their family situation and young children, in *Acta Psychiatrica Scandinavica* 90

Wates, M (2001) *Disabled parents and the 'young carers' issue.* Paper given at an NCH conference for young carers project workers, York 2001 www.DisabledParentsNetwork.org.uk

Wates, M. (2002) *Supporting Disabled Adults in their Parenting Role.* Joseph Rowntree Foundation

Wates, M. (2003) *It shouldn't be down to luck.* A report on a consultation with disabled parents for Disabled Parents Network. Full text, summary report and brief summary in plain English available from www.DisabledParentsNetwork.org.uk

Wates, M. (1997) *Disabled Parents: Dispelling the Myths.* National Childbirth Trust/Radcliffe Medical Press

Wates, M. and Jade, R. (1999) *Bigger than the Sky: Disabled Women on Parenting.* The Women's Press

Webster-Stratton, C. (1999) Researching the impact of parent training programmes on child conduct problems, in E. Lloyd (ed.) (1999) *Parenting Matters: what Works in Parenting Education?* Barnardo's

Weiner, M. (2002) *Understanding Deaf Parents with Hearing Children.* Paper presented at the 2nd International conference on disabled parenting, California 2002 and reviewed in *Disability, Pregnancy and Parenthood international* Journal 40(October)

White, C. and Barrowclough, C. (1998) Depressed and non-depressed mothers with problematic preschoolers: attributions for child behaviours, in *British Journal of Clinical Psychology* 37(4)

about the authors

Michele Wates is a writer, researcher and disabled parent. She is the Research Link for the Disabled Parents Network. She and Richard Olsen, Research Fellow in The Nuffield Community Care Studies Unit at the University of Leicester, both participated in the Joseph Rowntree Foundation Task Force aimed at improving support services to disabled parents in the UK. Richard and Michele have conducted a number of seminars with local authority personnel examining the historical impact of research on social policy in relation to disabled parents and the development of more integrated support for disabled adults with parenting responsibilities.

Michele Wates's other books and research reports include: *Disabled Parents: Dispelling the Myths* (NCT 1997), *Bigger than the Sky: disabled women on parenting* (The Women's Press 1999, Wates and Jade [eds]), *Supporting disabled adults in their parenting role* (Joseph Rowntree Foundation 2002) and *It shouldn't be down to luck*, report of a DPN consultation with disabled parents (DPN 2003). Michele Wates is currently preparing a rights handbook for Disabled Parents Network, to be published in 2004.

Richard Olsen's other work includes *Parenting and Disability: disabled parents' experiences of raising children* (published by the Policy Press in 2003) and a number of articles about 'young carers' (published in Disability and Society, 1996 and Children and Society, 2000). He currently convenes a series of ESRC-funded seminars for and about disabled parents at the University of Leicester.